Life in the Past Lane

Learning How to Focus Forward
Written by Rod Woitas

Life in the *Past* Lane

Learning How to Focus Forward
(Survival Guide)
Written by Rod Woitas

B.Ed., M.A. Counseling Psychology
Registered Psychologist
Registered Clinical Counsellor

TABLE OF CONTENTS

Right out of the gate I would like to thank my family and friends for all their support throughout the years. Lord knows we have had plenty of ups and downs, good and bad, successes and victories, setbacks, and heartaches.

Everything happens for a reason, and we do not, at the time, always understand 'the why' behind 'the what', but we can learn to be curious about the why and live and learn from the past and do a better job moving forward.

Key concepts in this book - learning how to focus forward on better days ahead, use evidence in your life to dispute negativity, and learning how to effectively communicate what you need and what that would look like within your relationship.

The arrow has left the bow. Life in the Past Lane is book number one, serving as an introduction to helpful strategies in a series of books written to help you live your best life.

Book number two, Killing the Toaster, will be released in the summer of 2022 and will expand on many of the strategies discussed in Life in the Past Lane as well as continue the adventures of Bill and Mary as they navigate through the challenges most married couples experience.

Stories have a beginning, a middle and an ending. This is how I structured this book. No chapters just an ongoing discussion about my life and the lived experiences of others. A journey with helpful strategies discussed throughout.

There are many strategies throughout this book that you may find helpful. If nothing else I hope it allows you to think about things in a different way and think about what you can do differently to make things better for you and your loved ones.

Please provide feedback to lifeinthepastlane2021@yahoo.com

INITIAL RANT

Life can be hard, sometimes much harder than it needs to be. This is not breaking news, especially during this difficult time we have all been trying to navigate through. Dealing with the present and worrying about the future is even more difficult and challenging when we are stuck in the past. We can agree that life should be better, and life should be easier but that is not always the case. We must try and make the best of each day we have, and not continue to be consumed by the negativity of our past.

We often grieve what should have been, and live life in the past lane. Living life in the past lane, simply stated, is when you cannot let go of past in order to appreciate the present and future. The goal is to focus forward on better days ahead. Focus forward on what you have to gain, not on what you may have lost.

We often get caught up in the "I should". I should have this; that should be me. You may have heard this at one time or another. For example, when that new Maserati drives by with the roar of the engine echoing down the street, "that should be me, that should be my car". My initial response to this statement is why? Why should you have this and why should that be you? What have you done to earn the things you covet so dearly?

Are you willing to put in the time and effort necessary to acquire those items or achieve those accomplishments? Faulty expectations regarding what you think you should have, lead to disappointments about what your currently have. There is a difference between wanting something and needing something. Think harder about what you need in your life versus what you want. This may say a lot about who you are. **What are the things you need versus the things you want? Make a list.**

Life is not a piece of cake and certainly, at times, it is not easy, but it is worth fighting the good fight every day to make your life and the life of others better. The negative people out there may have the attitude that life is more like a shit sandwich. So, its not enough that life's not easy and we complain about that, but life's also a shit sandwich. You have heard this all before. Negative people always complain about how hard life is and how unfair life is. Negative people might say something like this, "Yup, you get up in the morning and prepare to eat shit all day". This is bleak, to say the least, no glimmer of hope in that statement, and no possibility of breaking free from that negativity. If these people continue to dwell on that negative way of thinking about how the day will be, that will be how the day will be. This is so negative but so true for many struggling with anxiety, depression, stress, and relationship issues. I understand, sometimes its hard to see the positive, and sometimes even harder to care enough to look for it.

I have a bit of a laugh when I hear this comment come up. "I went into work today and it was a complete shit storm". Wow, how did you manage to cope with all that? I am still trying to figure out when using the word shit became so popular to describe life's struggles. Shit sandwich, shit burger, shit storm, losing my shit, "did you see Bill yesterday in that shit storm of a meeting, it was a buffet of shit sandwiches and shit burgers when Bill was losing his shit, what a shit show". Again, I say wow.

So, what do we do about all this negativity? How do we manage being around negative people? If nothing changes nothing changes. If you continue to be negative, then everything in and around you will also be negative. If you continue to surround yourself with negative people, it will affect who you are and how you are. Break free from this faulty belief system that life is awful, horrible, not worth living. Break free from hanging around people like this. I understand that there are many ups and downs in life and the road is often made of gravel not pavement.

What do we do on a gravel road? We slow down, become more aware, and make adjustments. This will be a key concept throughout this book. Take inventory of your thoughts and change them. Life can be great; you can have a great life if you choose to. The strategies in this book will help you get there.

INTRODUCTION

We have all heard the expression, time flies when you are having fun, and this is a true and accurate statement. However, time flies not only when you are having fun but also when you are busy or as we will discuss throughout this book, consumed with life. What you are busy with or focused on will also be an area of focus throughout this book. You will learn to be more aware and more willing to make adjustments in your life to get to a better place, instead of feeling stuck where you are.

It is amazing how fast time goes by as we age and especially when we are busy. I worked in education as a Teacher, Counsellor, Registered Psychologist, and Administrator. This would be 20 years of my life. As I will explain throughout this book, landing where I landed was truly not what I would have predicted for myself growing up.

Keep in mind as you read this book, life can change, life can get better. Maybe the place you are in right now is just a parking spot and you will be moving on soon or maybe this is where you are supposed to be. Only you can determine this. Time will tell and what you do during that time will determine whether this landing spot is permanent or temporary, and you have more of a journey to take.

As an educator, we had breaks built into our year so the pace of life is something we would take note of. We now had a fall, winter, and spring break, and of course the summer break. A friend suggested that when we get older, approximately 35 to 45 years of age, there is a chemical released in our brains that makes time seem to go by faster.

Now I want to mention here that my friend has no credentials that would qualify her to make a statement like this with any kind of accuracy and have not found supporting documentation to support her statement, but I cannot argue it because that is exactly how I feel. Where is the time going? The days, weeks, and months and even the years seem to be going by in a blink of an eye.

Others have commented that when you have children the clock seems to move faster, and the time goes by so quickly. Perhaps we are just so busy with all the duties we now have, or the routine of life is too consuming. I think it is fair to say that when you are busy time goes by faster. Also, when you are happy and enjoying your life, there never seems to be enough time with the people you care about most. Again, this seems to support the statement that time flies when you are having fun and keeping busy.

Time is going by so fast I cannot fully understand how I arrived at this place in my life. As I look at milestones in my life, a major event like high school graduation occurred 34 years ago. How is that possible? It has been 22 years since I graduated from university with my undergraduate degree and finally, it has been 26 years since I played football.

So why is it that I think I could put on my equipment tomorrow and be able to play? Why is it that I think University was just a few years ago? Why is it that the past consumes so many of us in the here and now distracting us from our future goals? **What are some of the milestones in your life that you can make note of from the past?**

Life in the Past Lane will explore anxiety, depression, relationships, the ups, and the downs, the good, the bad, and the ugly. I will explain why I believe we struggle with letting go of the past, why we focus on the negative, why we have some dysfunctional thoughts about how great life was "back in the day" when maybe it was not.

I believe this is part of the problem with letting go of the past or parts of the past because for a variety of different reasons we think it was so much better than it was. **What is it that you are holding onto from the past that is tripping you up today?**

I will provide some background on myself to hopefully give you a better understanding of where I am coming from. I will discuss my struggles with education, the great teachers I had, and the obstacles I overcame. I will discuss the social anxiety that I had to overcome and more specifically why we continue to be anxious about things we were anxious about when we were younger.

I will provide coping strategies I use with my clients so you can become empowered to make positive changes in your life. Strategies to overcome anxiety, depression, stress, and relationship issues.

Finally, I will discuss how we overcome this burden of reliving our past and continuing to be anxious, depressed or just stuck, making us feel overwhelmed about whether we will have a great life in the future. I will also provide questions for you to answer and reflect on as part of the work you can do to have a better life moving forward.

My thoughts, feelings, and opinions are based on my observations and personal experiences as a child, adolescent, and young adult living, at times, in a very dysfunctional home and growing up with limited guidance and support from others.

My observations as an educator, school counselor, and psychologist will provide a different perspective than most would hold. Leaning on the lived experiences of my life and the lived experiences of others I have worked with, provides me with more insight into the struggles we all have, and some of the solutions to the problems that we all hope to find.

I am not trying to say I am right and have all the answers to all our problems, but I believe that many are simply wrong in the way they focus on the negative and their negative past experiences. I am trying to provide you with perspective, a new and improved perspective on life, your life, and the life of others.

Think about it this way. In education we work with thousands of teenagers over the years. In the average family, you may have one or two or maybe three teenagers that you have direct contact with daily. It would stand to reason that educators would have more experience with teenagers than you do. For 15 years now I have been counselling children, adolescents, and adults. I can say I have experience with thousands of people's issues, problems, and concerns. This insight will help me help you.

Stories have a beginning, a middle and an ending. This is how I will structure the book, but the end of this story will be a new beginning for you as you focus forward on better days ahead.

By providing insight into the lived experiences of others, discussing strategies, and providing guidance and support, my hope for you is growth, change and an opportunity to become the best version of yourself. Our goal should always be to live and learn from our past and try and do a better job moving forward.

I sincerely hope you will enjoy this journey...

IN THE BEGINNING

I want you to write your birthdate down on a piece of paper. Take a good look at that date. It is the most important date in your life. Value that date and value yourself. You are here for a reason, and I want to help you identify that reason. July 14 is my important date. My birthday and the beginning of my story, and my journey into the unknown and uncertainties of my life.

Think about your own journey and where the twists and turns of life have taken you. Probably unpredictable and probably had many unknowns and uncertainties along the way. Our story and the stories of others have a beginning, a middle and an end and we want to explore these stories to have a better understanding of what we can do differently to make things better in our lives. **What can you do differently to make things better for you?**

Our stories are probably more similar than we may think. Obviously, the specific details may be different but fill in the blanks with your details and you will get what I mean. The early years of our story all seem to begin the same. We are born, we go home, but at this point our stories start to change. Think about your story as I tell you about mine.

I was born at the University of Alberta hospital located in Edmonton, Alberta and was brought home to the small town of Bruderheim, Alberta. Bruderheim is about an hour and a half Northeast of Edmonton. We lived on a farm outside of the city. I do not remember anything about this epic event but can only assume through reports that this is how it happened. I believe not remembering life at an early age is normal.

I think the memories we have about our early years are a mix of reality and fabricated memories we use to fill in some of the gaps. Some people will report that they remember being born, being one, being two and so on. I am not disputing they have some memories; I am just not convinced they are accurate memories of themselves at that age. The problem I see is we have too many competing stories that get confusing to the point where we do not know if that was our story or someone else's.

I talk to clients about being curious, looking for defining moments in life to help them gain a better understanding of why they are the way they are. Operating on this theme of being curious about defining moments, I had an opportunity to visit the old homestead a few years ago. It was interesting to drive down the old gravel road and approach the old house. I was anticipating a rush of memories but, unfortunately, I did not.

I guess part of me was hoping to reveal something about myself that I had not previously known. I would often have dreams as a young child, being in a kitchen, in a house with my mother. That is my only memory of the house but as I said when I was there, standing in the kitchen, it stirred up zero emotion. Most likely I had fabricated some memories of what I thought it was like living there as a small child. I would like you to continue to think about your story as I continue mine. **What stands out for you? What defining moments can you make note of?**

When I was two years old my mother divorced my biological father and moved to the City of Edmonton to raise my brothers and me. For some, this is already the formula for dysfunction. In the 1970s, if you were a child from a broken home the so-called experts at that time said you were destined for drugs, alcohol and a life of misery and heartache. This could have been our story, a single mother with 3 boys moving to the big city. How could anything good come from this?

Already, the path for us would be much different than many others at that time. I was the youngest of three. My brothers were older than me by 5 and 7 years. They were much closer with each other than they were with me, so I do not have a lot of warm and fuzzy stories to tell you about us all hanging out and having fun. They did their own thing and participated in activities like the Cub Scouts, and I honestly cannot remember what else they might have been doing.

I also do not remember what I was doing either. I know I was alone most of the time. I would wander around a lot, would ride my bike a lot but other than that I do not remember much more. As I mentioned my brothers were older than me and had more of a life at that time than I did.

When working with my clients who may be suffering from negativity in their lives, I use a strategy I call the blueprint for success. Paying attention and taking note of the things that are going well in their life and documenting these things. Things like how they act, how they respond to others, who they are with, what activities are they engaged in and so on.

Basically, documenting why things are going well at that time when things are going well. This is your blueprint for success. These are things you want to remember so when things go sideways you have a better idea of what you can do to pull yourself back on track, rather than continue your slide deeper into a pool of negativity. **What can you put down on your blueprint for success?**

So far in my life I did not have a lot to put down on my blueprint for success. Living with my mother and two brothers and being alone most of the time is a lonely place to be, but as I say to my clients "sometimes you have to look over the fence and down the road to see what's there instead of focusing on the here and now".

Imagine this, you are sitting in your backyard, and you have a fence all around you. All you really see is the fence. In other words, all you get to see is what is directly in front of you and if that is not good then all you see or all you focus on is the negative. If you are not careful, you become consumed with negativity, but here is another strategy that may help.

I suggest creating more awareness and more of a willingness to make an adjustment in your life. If you have an opportunity to look over the fence and down the street, you open opportunities to bring in new information that may help you. Be aware and then make an adjustment. I believe there is always hope for better days ahead, sometimes you may need to fight harder to see the light at the end of the tunnel or look over the fence, and down the street to see what else is there.

Not being close with my brothers would be a theme that continues today. There was a short period when we did connect a little bit but that was many years ago and as life gets busy, we often focus more on our own journey and sometimes get our priorities out of order and do not pay attention to the journeys of our loved ones.

I do believe family and friends should come before work, but we all get stuck in this trap at one time or another and as I will say often throughout this book, we need to have awareness and a willingness to make adjustments to live our best lives. **Are there people in your life you need to reconnect with?**

Looking back now, I must admit my mother showed a lot of courage to leave her husband back in the 1970s, when leaving husbands was not the thing to do. As you are aware times have changed. Now a disagreement over butter or margarine can result in divorce. We are not putting in enough time and effort to build and grow our relationships and that is why so many are failing.

Perhaps part of that faulty belief system we discussed earlier that life should be easy, relationships should be easy, achieving success in life should be easy. However, as we gather evidence in our lives, we know that time and effort is necessary to have successful relationships just as time and effort is necessary for us to achieve success in our work lives. Life is not easy, but it can be better than it is right now.

I do not remember many emotionally charged events in detail from my earlier years. I thought maybe I was somehow blocking it out, but really, I think like many others I just have not sat down and thought about it enough. I have a general recollection of the events but no deep, emotional attachments to specific events seem to be present for me.

Even as I write this, you would think it would be a perfect time to reflect and think about my past more, but again, the events that come up are not emotionally charged in any way. I have a theory about this. I say to clients, and not to minimize their experiences but, your past is over, we cannot go back in time, that was then, and this is now. Take what you can from the past to help you have a better life in the future.

In other words, I have taken what I can from my past to help me have a better future. So, I am not blocking out the past, I have already in one way, or another, taken the information I felt was useful and have moved on. Live and learn from the past and try to do a better job moving forward.

The fact that I have not identified any emotionally charged events is okay. Again, that was then, and this is now and if you are happy with where you are in your life currently then how much does it really matter. If you are unhappy with where you are right now this would be a time for you to dive in and do more reflection on what was going on at that time, the defining moments, the time you remember when things were going well to the time when things stopped going well. **Is something from your past holding you back from enjoying your life in the here and now and holding you back from embracing thoughts about happiness in the future? Write down your thoughts on this.**

We are not in denial that there has been negativity in our lives. I believe we all have something we are trying to work through. We want to address these concerns and look at our most recent evidence in our lives to dispute the negativity. We want to dispute negativity with evidence it will be okay. This is another key strategy that will be discussed throughout.

I remember my mother being gone most of the time. My grandmother was the one who watched us while my mother worked. No one could ever dispute how hard my mother worked. She did so much during those years to support us and made so many sacrifices to keep us in a house with food on the table.

As children, during the early years, we do not fully comprehend the sacrifices our parents are making for us. I believe if we were more aware we probably would have helped more. Working with clients I stress the importance of having balance in their lives, work hard to provide for your families but make sure you have some balance. We work to live, not live to work.

An exercise I do with clients is having them make a list of their priorities in life. I am interested in where they put work on their list. Here is an example I use with my clients. If you believe in God then we put God as number one, then your spouse, then your children, then extended family and friends, then activities you may enjoy, then work. Notice where work showed up on this list.

Work was number six on the list but many of us live life like it is number one. This is a mistake we all make, and therefore I talk about awareness and a willingness to make adjustments. Once we are aware that our priorities are in the wrong order, we need to make an adjustment. When we are faced with a decision in our lives think about whether that decision will have a negative or a positive impact on our priorities. This can help guide your decision making.

Life can be challenging, it can be hard, it can even be overwhelming, but it can also be amazing if we focus on the right things, if we identify our priorities in life (family and friends) and think about how our decisions in life will impact our priorities.

"You will define your success in your own way. That is not for me or anyone else to decide. You, yourself, will define your own success in your own way."

The struggles of a single mother with three boys meant that sometimes my mother needed to lean on the resources she had in her life to help us get through. There were times when uncles and aunts would help. That is why building, and growing relationships is so important. At different times in our lives, we may need support.

So, with the support of family and some friends my mother found a way to make it through her day to day. What I can tell you or what I want you to take from this is life does not have to be perfect from the start for you to be successful or to achieve success. You will define your success in your own way. That is not for me or anyone else to decide. You, yourself, will define your own success in your own way.

Some roads we choose to travel are bumpy and rough, made of gravel, and some are smooth and paved, but either way we need to stay focused forward on better days ahead and continue to do the things we need to do to arrive at our desired destination.

My beginnings were not necessarily favorable, but I had, despite all the looming dysfunction, people around me that cared, and this is a key ingredient for having some sense of security in this world. Just because I felt alone most of the time does not mean there was no one around to support me if needed.

Often children feel alone because they do not know where they fit in this world. Our job as parents and the job of other adults in a child's life is to show children where they fit, show children they have value and worth. Where do we fit in this world?

Look at the world as a gigantic puzzle. Each one of us is a puzzle piece. The picture can not be completed without us, without you. Some of us may be on the edges and some of us may be right in the middle, but either way the picture cannot be completed without us. We may play a different role and that is okay because regardless of our role we have value in the big picture. This concept may be extremely useful when someone is feeling alone, sad, depressed and wondering where they fit in this world and whether its worth continuing in this world.

There is a statement I will make later about pay now or pay later and it is the point I will make here as well. Put in the time and effort early on or you will have more issues and problems down the road.

We must invest in our children at an early age and continue to invest and support them well into adulthood. This type of support is missing today, and we need to find a way to make this a priority. **What can you do differently to make your loved ones feel like they are a priority?**

I am not sure I had anyone investing in me or supporting me in a way that stood out. My brothers went to school, and I stayed home with my grandmother while my mother worked. That is the amount of investment I remember but as I have mentioned earlier, just because that is how I remember it does mean that is how it was.

We need to be careful about making assumptions about how life was or how people were. We often assume what people think, how they may react or what they may do. As I often say to my clients, if we are making too many assumptions about something it is an indication that we need to communicate more.

My perception of the past may also be distorted. I may have fabricated some memories to fill in some of the gaps but being curious about our past can reveal more about who we are. Instead of making an assumption about my past and a lack of support that may or may not be true I decided to explore some of my past to see if I could gather some relevant information to get some answers to my questions.

I recently visited our old neighborhood and drove by the old school my brothers went to. I was curious about the name of the school and curious what the old neighborhood looked like. I was surprised because this school was one that I had to go back to while I was doing my undergraduate degree in education. It is now an outdoor education center.

Of course, when I was there doing my university course work for outdoor education, I had no idea this was the school my brothers attended. I am always amazed at how often the past comes full circle and hits us in the face during the here and now. How we cope and manage with the past and the impact we allow the past to have on us will be discussed in more detail later.

I am also amazed at some of the memories we have and the ones we see value in. As a small child, I remember wandering off a lot. One time there was a huge house fire down the street from us. I remember walking down the street and climbing to the top of a hill to watch the action. Firetrucks, lights, people from the neighborhood, it was awesome. One of those moments that sticks with you.

The problem with this was no one knew where I was. Looking back, it is clear I contributed to some of the panics my grandmother and mother experienced back then. Perhaps this was the beginning of their anxiety disorders.

My point here is we seek out excitement, action, something to distract us. I call this a healthy distraction. The things in our lives that help us not to overthink or over analyze every move we make. Sitting on top of a hill watching several firefighters put out a fire is one of those unique, specific, and maybe not so healthy distractions that allowed me to escape from whatever else I may have been going through at that time. If I were to guess, currently in my young life, I was probably lonely, and this was a way for me to feel like I was a part of something.

Other times I remember going off into the river valley following a narrow path, up a hill thick with trees. At the top, there was an open field and a building where my brothers went to Cub Scouts. Considering the neighborhood and the thick forest, it is amazing I was not afraid.

I believe children today know better than to leave and wander off without permission or without a parent or guardian around to protect them. Nowadays I believe we deliver more messages that cause our children to be afraid and I get it, there are bad people out there that do bad things.

We should also deliver messages that there are amazing people in our world and once we have built some trust with these people, they contribute to us feeling safe and secure in this world. I will talk more about this during our discussion about creating our inner circles.

I did not know better and wandered off all the time and as I have said, this was most likely my version of a healthy distraction, my way of keeping my mind busy. Maybe being able to wander off was also a sign of the times, a time when children were safe or had less fear of the world around them.

As I reflect further, I remember some reports of bodies found in the thick brush so maybe it was not so child friendly after all. Now remember I mentioned reality versus fabricated memories. I cannot say with 100% confidence that there were bodies found in the bushes but that is what I remember.

It is interesting to reflect on my story at this point and acknowledge that I do not recall any positive memories other than recognizing that there were people in my life that cared.

Overall, I think we were just in survival mode. Trying to make the best of a bad situation or maybe it was not bad at all. I guess it all depends on what or who you are comparing your life to and again interpreting what reality was and what was the fabricated memories you have chosen to carry forward. **Are the memories you have chosen to carry forward helping you or hurting you in your quest for a happy life?**

We lived in a little black and white house. I remember it being small but fitting in with the rest of the houses on the block. My mother ran the show.

She was and still is a very independent woman. She organized us and kept us alive as she worked full time to support us.

If my mother was overwhelmed or stressed, I certainly did not know about it. We lived in the river valley, which now is prime real estate, but back then I think my mothers' motivation was to be close to downtown where she worked. She never had any high paying jobs in her life, always making just enough for us to get by.

My mother met my stepfather when I was around five years old. They got married and we moved to a new house in Castledowns. Castledowns is located on the north side of Edmonton. I remember when we initially went to look at the house, I ran across the construction site, stepped on a nail, and had to go to the hospital for a tetanus shot. Another great memory.

Anyway, the house was okay, about 1000 square feet. It was a typical 3-bedroom bungalow. Looking back this could be perceived as a glimmer of hope. We would be a family in a house, but I am not sure this even mattered to me at my age. I had other childhood things to focus on like school and friends and where I would ride my bike next.

A big mistake I feel we make nowadays is assuming our young children are going through the adult ups and downs of life or the emotional rollercoaster of life that we as adults are experiencing. I do not believe this is true. I know it was not true for me.

I did not care what was going on. All I knew is we were moving to a new house. I had no idea about adult concerns that may have been present. As a therapist I have had many conversations with adults who have reported that as a child they were not necessarily aware of everything that was going on but now can clearly describe the dysfunction they were exposed to as children. So, when we are ready to do this, I believe we can recall the ups and downs of childhood and work towards making more sense of it all. This is us using our adult brains.

Finding that defining moment from our past can help you gain an under-standing of how, why, what, and who you are or have become but as I have suggested, as a child I believe we are mostly concerned with being a child. Let your children be children. Do not overwhelm them with your adult concerns.

The new house was in a new area, so all the school-aged children were bussed out of the community to go to school because our community school was still under construction. I have confusing memories about this time. We did not ride the typical yellow school bus; we rode the city busses. The Edmonton Transit Service (ETS). This was scary for a six-year-old. The bus had regular people on it, not just students.

I remember missing my stop on occasion and becoming completely lost somewhere along the route. As a young child, I was easily distracted so the fact that I was daydreaming on a bus on my way to school is not surprising to me. I remember one time as I was wandering around looking for my school a man in a 'student driver' car picked me up.

He was a nice man who asked me if I was lost and if he could help me. I told him yes, I was lost, and I told him the name of my school. He drove me to school in his 'student driver' car. I remember this because on the passenger side floor there was a brake pedal. I guess in case one of his students went out of control during a lesson he could apply this brake and save them from having an accident.

As I reflect on this it makes me wonder what kind of a world we were living in when it was okay for a six-year-old to get on a city bus alone to go to school miles away from his community. On the one hand, it worked out okay, no harm, no foul.

I also understand my parents were busy working so they were just doing what they could to make sure we made it to school. I have no idea or mem-ory of where my brothers were at this time. Were they on the bus and sitting somewhere away from me? Were they on a different bus? They were older than me so it would make sense if their bus were different than mine.

One of the things I remember about this time is the kindness of strangers. It seemed like countless bus drivers and good samaritans helped me find my way to school on different occasions. That whole "it takes a village to raise a child" philosophy must have been in play, and I am a firm believer in being available to help others.

We need to do a better job of supporting and understanding each other. We live in a truly diverse world, and we must do better at being more available to help others.

I can remember the old school quite clearly. The neighborhood was old and tough and there were often fights between rival schools. Not something you hear about now adays, but it seemed to be a regular occurrence back then. After a year or so at this older school, located outside of our community, we were able to move to our new school in our new community as construction was now completed.

It was exciting to be in a new school and a bit of a relief that it was close to our home. That being said, I was not a good student at all. Not academically, not behaviorally. I had no one at home to help guide me through my studies or even ask me how school was going. Both my parents were working, and both my parents seemed too always be busy.

A lesson for all the parents out there, be present for your children and help them, and when you ask them how school was and they say good and walk away, ask them why it was good. Try and expand the conversation as much as you can and as often as you can. Teach your children the importance of communication.

An odd memory from that time stands out. I can remember other students knowing how to tell time. I remember thinking that their parents must have put in the time and effort to help them otherwise how did they know. Maybe this was my way of justifying my lack of ability to tell time.

Until that moment, I had no idea parents did this, so the saying "you don't know what you don't know" would seem to fit here. All I remember is my parents worked. They worked, paid bills, and fought just about all the time.

I can recognize this now and as I reflect; I can identify a shift from when I remembered little about the dysfunction of my family to a time when I can clearly remember almost all of it. I believe this is part of growing up and becoming more aware.

Again, no emotionally charged memories, just memories. I would say this defining moment happened when I was around six or seven. School, friends, and exposure to other children's lives revealed to me how different my situations were. Before this I had no idea, now I was beginning to see there was something a bit off with our situation, I was becoming more aware.

> "Good teachers don't just teach the curriculum they help expand our horizons, so we become more aware of the world around us."

I remember a school field trip into downtown Edmonton. On a couple of occasions', we went as a class to see movies. Movies like Star Wars and Ben-Hur, two epic films. Ben-Hur makes me curious because if I remember correctly, it was a film from 1959, we were elementary age students.

Someone must have known the value of all this, I am not sure I did but that is where our teachers come in. Good teachers do not just teach the curriculum they help expand our horizons, so we become more aware of the world around us. I will talk about this more later but want to mention it now, the teachers in my life were amazing. The opportunities they gave me were amazing and as I have said, teachers do not just teach the curriculum, they help expand our horizons.

I remember riding back to the school on the bus. I was staring out the window lost in my world. Looking back, I was probably depressed but at the time who knows what I was. No one ever asked how I was feeling. I remember the teacher praising my behavior. They were so pleased they did not have to deal with behavioral issues on this trip.

The fact that they noticed me and provided me with some positive reinforcement is powerful. That would have been approximately 45 years ago, and I still remember it. If you are a teacher, remember how powerful your words are, the words and actions you use have a profound effect on your students.

When I was in grade five my mother divorced my stepfather. I remember lots of conflict in the house, lots of yelling. I remember a counselor coming to the house to talk to me about how I felt about the situation. I remember saying everything was okay. Why would I say such a thing when I knew there was fighting almost every day?

Even to this day, this scenario seems like such an odd thing to do to a young boy, asking about conflict in the house. What I remember from this time was I often prepared the couch for my mother to sleep on. I did not see this as a slight against my stepfather. I was just trying to be nice to my mother.

Looking back, I can see how this might have been viewed negatively by my stepfather, but it was not my fault. I could not possibly take responsibility for my parents' conflicts. I say this because I know a lot of children and adolescents blame themselves for their parent's conflict, separations, and divorces.

To the children and adolescents out there let me say this to you, do not do that, do not ever blame yourself, it is not your fault. Sometimes adults have conflicts, sometimes these conflicts can be resolved, sometimes they cannot, and they choose to separate or divorce.

I know sometimes we feel as children and adolescents that the world revolves around us and everything has something to do with us, but this is a case where the adult stuff is just the adult stuff. It honestly has nothing to do with you. As I write this, I can say Alberta has some of the highest divorce rates in all of Canada, not a statistic to be proud of.

Another important event to note around this time and unfortunately another negative event. I came home from school one day and my mother was home sitting at the kitchen table crying. I asked her what was wrong, she said your father died today. Not my stepfather, but my biological father that she divorced when I was two. I did not know him at any time in my life, so this did not have much of an impact on me.

Talk to your children so you can have a better understanding of what they are going through because they are not always going through the same emotional rollercoaster you are going through. I have said a couple times throughout already, I did not have a lot of emotionally charged memories from the past but this one is a little bit different.

It bothered me a bit more as I got older. I think a part of me wanted to know my biological father. Who was he? How was he? What did he sound like? Was he a nice guy that helped others? Again, as I got older this bothered me more. A missing piece in my puzzle that I could never fill.

When my parents (mother and stepfather) decided to divorce, my mother and I moved into co-op housing. This was for low-income families. It was a two-bedroom townhouse so enough room for me and my mother.

My two older brothers stayed with my stepfather. They were at the age where they could choose where they lived and probably more out of convenience made the choice to stay. I was not old enough to choose or even comprehend what was going on, but I remember the move.

It was odd, to say the least. I was now leaving my home. It makes me sad to think about this now but at the time I guess I just kept everything inside. It is hard to express emotion about something you have no understanding of. What did all this mean? At the time I knew I did not know.

Now I can see that my mother's independent ways and my stepfather's inability to communicate effectively led to conflicts that could not be resolved. When I work with couples now, I emphasize the importance of communication and use a communication, understanding, support model.

It goes like this. I could not support you unless I understood what you were going through, and I could not understand what you are going through unless you told me. Communication leads to understanding, which leads to support. Simple concept but we all tend to mess this one up. I will discuss this more in a different section focused on couples counseling.

As I mentioned our community school was completed and the low-income housing was located just across the field so no more scary bus rides for me. I remember the way the teachers reacted to the news that my parents had separated. They had no clue how to manage me. I was already a "difficult" student but now there seemed to be valid reasons for my rebellion.

"My teachers in elementary school allowed me to have a life at school when there was no real positive life away from school."

I remember running down the hallway with my friend, he was slightly ahead of me as we came closer to our classroom, so I pushed him from behind, he went flying into the wall, putting his knee right through the drywall. I did not get in trouble, nothing, not a thing.

Back then I had no idea what this lack of consequence meant. I just remember the worker fixing the hole and that was the end of it. I now realize that my teachers were sparing me from any additional heartache. My teachers paid attention to me and provided positive reinforcement whether I was good or bad. They allowed me to be a part of activities even if I did not earn the right. My teachers in elementary school allowed me to have a life at school when there was no real positive life away from school.

I found emotional connections with educators who cared, and it never mattered how busy they were, they were always there when I needed them. My elementary school teachers (at both schools) provided me with enough support to give me a fighting chance for success in my future.

My teachers saw something that was worth saving and I cannot thank them enough. I knew nothing about myself or how life would play out for me, and I believe this is the point parents and teachers need to realize.

Children and even adolescents are desperate for guidance. We need to connect with them somehow, some way, because they do not know what is going on. They do not have the life experience or wisdom to make the right choices or to fully understand what life all is about, what the big picture is or could be. Some suggest that adolescents can only really look a few months ahead at a time. Perhaps for some, this is true.

When I was a child, I played football, hockey, and baseball. This I believe was my mother's way of keeping me out of trouble. I think it worked. If I was involved in activity, keeping busy, staying focused on something I enjoyed, I was great.

The experts agree with this point. Keep your children in organized sport or a healthy activity and you will see a decrease in unwanted behavioral issues. This does not mean they do not need supervision, guidance, and support but it helps them feel more connected with the world around them. It helps them build and grow new relationships.

For the most part activities kept me out of trouble, although I do remember taking bus trips to downtown Edmonton with my friends, which may not seem like a big deal but when you are around 10 years old wandering around downtown Edmonton late at night this is not something adults would approve of.

As I mentioned before, children and adolescents desperately require guidance from adults, and if there is no guidance children and adolescents just make it up as they go along based on some of the information they have gathered from their observations of others.

When it came to sports, I was the type of kid that focused on being the best I could be. As a baseball player, I played first base and could catch anything thrown my way. I also pitched, played back catcher and outfielder.

I was good at baseball but probably the only 10 years old to throw his arm out. I could not believe it. Why was I having so much difficulty with my arm? Was I throwing too hard? Throwing the wrong way? No one investigated this. Not a big deal. I really enjoyed baseball and made some good friends during my time playing. This was a great distraction for me at a time when some of my other friends were beginning to get into trouble.

I do appreciate the guidance of my coaches. The father figures I did not have in my life at home. My coaches did not realize how much they impacted me because I was not emotionally equipped to show them my appreciation for their efforts.

The coaches probably saved me more than I realize and as I have said, probably more than they realize. Without them, I would have, without a doubt, traveled down a path of negativity like experimenting with drugs or other high-risk behaviors.

The friends I had that were not involved in sports were involved in drugs and that is all they cared about. They thought they were cool because they did what they wanted whenever they wanted, and I was a loser because I had to be on time for practice and refused to miss to hang out with them. I believe I made the right choice.

Unsupervised, unsupported children make poor choices. I mentioned my friend from elementary. I saw him again when I was in high school, and he was now a mess. Incredibly sad to see someone like this. Back when we were in elementary his cousin introduced him to drugs. This friend took so much acid over the years that he was a complete mess by the time he hit high school. His brain was gone.

He was functioning at the level of a 5-year-old. What a waste of a life and all because of drugs and choices and associating with someone who just wanted someone to get high with. I tell a story about a group of teenagers at school, on the corner smoking during breaks and at lunch.

If one teenager is out there, they may realize that what they are doing is wrong. If 10 teenagers are out there, they think everyone is doing it so what is the problem. Mob mentality. The minority acts like they are the majority. This is how dangerous peer pressure is. Teenagers just want to be a part of something, and it really does not matter if its good and positive or bad and negative the point is to feel like they belong somewhere, and they fit somewhere. **What are you doing to make your child or teenager feel like they belong in your home?**

Again, I stress the importance of getting your children involved in positive activities like sports, music, volunteering, something, anything, it is life changing. The other thing that bothered me about my friend's situation was the fact that this friend had great parents. They had a nice house, and lots of money but obviously, there is more to this than I knew. Something was off and perhaps my friend did not feel like he belonged in his own home.

I often say people allow you to see what they want you to see. It is a façade, superficial, not the real deal. The example I use with clients is a nice family playing at the park. They are laughing and playing and having fun. You compare your situation to theirs and start feeling upset or angry because you want this but do not have it.

What we typically do in this situation is blame the people around us for our own failures to do something different to make things better. Stop doing this! Take responsibility for your own story and change it. Do not compare your story to a story you know nothing about. You know nothing about this picture you are comparing yourself to. With the example of the family playing in the park, this could be one positive frame in the movie, and you just happen to see it. Not fair to you or your family.

These external factors cause stress and heartache, we must stop doing this. Again, people allow you to see what they want you to see. I caution my clients about comparing themselves to other people because as I have said, people allow you to see what they want you to see, and they tell you what they want you to know.

You will define your success in your own way, and this is true about your family dynamics. If seeing a happy family helps you hope for better days and motivates and drives you to do better than great, but if it makes you angry and envious then you are missing the point I am trying to make here. Write your own story. Make it what you want it to be. Sit down with your partner and develop a shared vision moving forward. **What story will you write?**

Returning to our discussion about healthy activities for our children and adolescents. I want to continue with my next adventure, the sport of hockey. Hockey was awesome. I remember how that all played out. One night I was cutting through some yards to get home quicker, it was dark and late, and I was in trouble. We had a rule and some of you might remember this one. Be home before the streetlights come on. Well, they were on, and I was late.

While cutting through one of those houses, in the dark, crossing through a yard, I was confronted by a boy yelling "hey what are you doing". I knew this voice, in fact, I knew the boy. It was the hockey coaches' son. I did what any other boy would have done in my position; I said "hey, I was planning on playing hockey, do you know if your dad is home". Lame I know but it worked. I did not get in trouble.

The problem now was I just joined a hockey team and I did not know how to skate. I never had anyone to take me out and teach me, but I also never asked so if you do not communicate what you need and what that would look like, people will not understand what you need and what that would look like and therefore cannot support you the way you need them too.

I know that was a lot of words to say if you do not ask you will never know. I think my silence was probably a major contributor to how my relationship would be with my parents. We can say they should have known but I also could have asked.

Remember, communication, understanding, support. This model is highly effective when dealing with any relationship in your life. Remember that people cannot read your mind, they do not know what you are thinking or what you may want. Work harder to communicate more effectively.

Returning home from my adventure cutting through yards and joining hockey, I broke the news to my parents. To their credit, they followed up and officially registered me for hockey, they bought me skates and all the equipment necessary to begin this new adventure. I went out to the local outdoor rink with some friends that already played hockey, and I learned how to skate and shoot a puck. I was ready.

I played hockey for about six years. I started as a defenseman but ended up as a goalie. I was an incredibly good goalie, MVP at several tournaments, good enough to catch the attention of the club teams but I was lazy and did not have a strong work ethic at that time and again at this time had no one around to guide me, no one to push me to do more, or work harder. I would get dropped off and picked up at hockey practices and games (parents please do not do this-put in some effort).

I believe for all of us, if we are willing to put in the time and effort, we can accomplish anything. Being lazy and not understanding the importance of putting in time and effort did not get me far.

A prime of example of this was the time I made a double-A hockey team that was several steps up from the community league team. This did not last long because I did not have the drive to work hard and improve every day.

This was a lost opportunity for me. I think about it this way now. If my parents would have stayed and watched me during a practice and witnessed how I would skate hard when the coach was watching and then coast when he was not, perhaps they would have said something helpful to make me realize I needed to do more if I wanted to be successful.

I now realize that you need to be motivated and driven to have success and sometimes you need someone in your life to push you along. Coaches can only do so much. Perhaps if the coaches knew more about my situation they would have helped more.

It is odd because when my involvement in sports began my parents were together but somewhere in between they divorced. I do not know if anyone knew this.

I tell my clients how important communication is. The model I use, as I mentioned earlier, is Communication-Understanding-Support and because it is so valuable, I will explain it again. I could not support you if I did not understand what you were going through, and I would never know what you are going through unless you told me, unless you communicated with me.

I should have communicated more but I did not know how to. Once you get used to no one listening, you start to shut down and withdraw and give up trying to communicate with others. Sooner or later, you stop trying.

If someone comes to you with a problem or an issue and you continually reject them, they will stop coming. This is a learned behavior. **Is there someone in your life that you have been shutting down, shutting out? What can you do differently to make this better?**

Football was the game that changed my life and again just like hockey it was by accident that I was introduced to the game. I remember getting off the bus one afternoon and some friends were playing football on a field by the bus stop. I went over to take a closer look. They asked me if I wanted to play. I said sure.

I remember one boy handing the ball off to me and me running and running and running. Not zigzagging but running straight and fast (remember Forrest Gump). No one could catch me. I heard the boys talking amongst themselves, something like "should we ask him, should we tell him"?

The thing they were talking about was the bantam football tryouts. I had absolutely no idea about this but thought why not? I asked my mom and she said that there was no way she was going to let me play.

I know I heard the words but as I mentioned earlier, I was not a great listener so every day during the summer when my mother went off to work, I would ride my bike across town to participate in the football tryouts.

Back then the age limits were from 12-15 years old, I was 10. I never missed a single practice even though I never was issued equipment or was ever officially on the team. I did not participate in hitting drills but did everything else, including hitting the sleds. I did this for 2 full seasons.

Some of the older boys used to ask me "what are you doing here?" I would reply "football practice, I'm here for football practice". They could not understand why I was doing what I was doing but I knew I found something real. Looking back, they were bullies trying to break me, break my spirit but I was too naive to even understand that I was being bullied. Looking back the coaches must have also seen the value in allowing me to participate.

When I turned 12, I was issued equipment for the first time. It was awesome, no more bruises on my shoulders from hitting the sleds with no equipment. They put me at middle linebacker. I had no idea what that was because all I ever did was run through the drills for 2 years, I never really learned any positions.

With some guidance, I slowly learned what was going on. I remember my first game ever. The running back came through the line and laid a massive hit on me, almost knocked me out. The funny thing about that was the running back was a girl, long ponytail flopping down from her helmet. I did not care; I was just wondering where the huddle was. I guess this was concussion number one.

> *"A message I try and deliver to client is, I would rather go all in on something and fail then take the easy road and always wonder what if."*

I ended up playing a couple of years with the Safeway Seals (officially a couple of years, remember I had two years with no equipment). I started to get very good. I received MVP, and a head-hunter award for aggressive play, I was on to something now.

I dropped baseball and hockey and put all my focus on football. Now I did this despite having success in all three but sometimes we need to make choices in our life to help us learn and grow and discover what might be.

In other words, go all in on something and let the chips fall where they may. All or nothing, and oddly enough, this is one of the things we want to avoid when we are working with clients suffering from anxiety. All or nothing thinking is not healthy, but in this scenario, it seemed to make sense to drop the other sports to focus on this one.

A message I try and deliver to client is, I would rather go all in on something and fail then take the easy road and always wonder what if. I never really wonder about baseball, but I do think about hockey on occasion but as I have said earlier, we want to live and learn from our past and do a better job moving forward. I learned from hockey that I needed to work harder, do more, and put in time and effort if I wanted to be successful. Live and learn and do a better job moving forward.

The next level in football was high school, and I was ready. My mother knew about football at this point, hard to keep a secret that long. In total, all in, I played 18 years of football and my mother came to 2 games.

I have an important message for all the parents reading this book, go to your children's games. You are missing out. You can never allow yourself to get so busy that you are not involved in your children's life. Pay now or pay later. Paying now is positive and fun, paying later can be pure hell as your child makes blind, uneducated, unguided choices and ends up on drugs and on the streets.

Honestly, this happens all the time, do not fool yourself into thinking your little son or daughter is immune to this, they are not. They are one bad choice away from ruining their lives and you need to be there to help them, to guide them. I was lucky, most kids are not. They get sucked in and rebel, push back and get into trouble.

This is when parents come to me and ask what they can do. I say what have you done to guide and support them at 6, 8, and 10? Were you involved in their lives or were you too busy working or consumed with your own issues, problems, and concerns? There is no shortcut to raising your children. Spending time with your children is the most important contribution you can make to their lives. You cannot build and grow a relationship if you are never around to build and grow the relationship.

Alright, back to football. As I mentioned, the most valuable player on my bantam football team gave me some confidence to continue despite older and not necessarily wiser people telling me I was too small to play.

One father of a girl I knew in high school told me to forget about football He went on to explain that my bone structure was too small, whatever that meant. Some adults should just shut up. Why be negative, why make someone feel bad, sad, or discouraged. Deal with your issues and problems so you do not spew your negativity onto others who are just trying to have some glimmer of hope that life is worth living. Words are powerful.

> *"We need to listen to what our children are telling us, be involved, and show some compassion. Have a heart, lead with your heart, make an emotional connection with your children."*

Comments can be daggers to the heart. This guy had no idea about me or my life or what I had overcome thus far. There are so many different layers to us, so many different stories. We need to be careful about what we say to others because we have no idea how they are or who they are or where they came from and if they are emotionally equipped to cope with the negative bullshit, you are throwing their way.

It upsets me because adults do this all the time. Throwing out advice based on their own miserable experiences of life. Think before you speak. Are you saying what you are saying to be helpful and encouraging or are you a bitter, angry person who is out to hurt others because you have been hurt? As I said, think before you speak.

I talked about communication earlier and how important it is to be involved in your children's life. I stand by that 100% if you are not destroying your child's hopes and dreams. We do not have to be the ones to trip up our children or to criticize them.

Yes, be realistic, but watch what and how you say what you are saying. It is not always the message that is the problem but often the delivery of the message. There are enough bad people out there that will be negative, discouraging, and critical. You do not have to be one of them. We need to listen to what our children are telling us, be involved, and show some compassion. Have a heart, lead with your heart, make an emotional connection with your children.

I have had many cases over the years that are related to this type of negative undermining. Here is an example I use: You grow up doing the best you can, putting in time and effort and really focused on making good choices and staying focused forward. You bring home your exam results or your report card and what do you get? If you are receiving 80's your parents say well if you can get 80's why not 90's, you come home with 90's and they say if you can get 90's why not 100's. Nothing you do is every good enough. This message sticks with us so even when we achieve success its never seems like enough. The old tape is still playing.

The negative things we hear from others, the negative thoughts we continually have and dwell on changes us. It changes how we feel, how we behave and tears apart our self esteem, self confidence and self worth. The point here is, even when we are successful and doing all the things we need to be doing, and from the outside looking in you have a great life, you are still not happy. Nothing makes you happy. You are incapable of being happy and you do not know why. Negative comments and negative thoughts undermine our abilities to succeed.

All that to get here. As I said, when adults discourage children, I get upset about this because I had to overcome a lot of that at a young age. I know what it feels like to do all I could and have someone say, yes but what about this.

Once we are older, we are more aware, and we can make or should make adjustments when we are faced with this negativity. We can stay stuck or use this information to help motivate and drive us to do more.

In high school, they called me "Mr. Football". All I ever focused on was working out and playing football, nothing else mattered and to be honest I did not have a lot more going on at the time. As I have said before, if you are willing to put in the time and effort you can accomplish anything. Do not let someone else write your story. Write your own story.

I remember my teachers; I remember all my teacher throughout my education. They were strict and provided structure, but they were also adults who cared enough to ask me how I was doing? No one else in my life other than my coaches ever asked me this question. My teachers guided me through adolescents. They offered up advice and told me things I may not have wanted to hear but needed to hear. They cared enough to step in and make a difference, so I was not left alone to make my own misguided decisions.

Teachers contributed more to who I am today than any other adults in my life and many of the children who went through difficult times could probably say the same thing. Whether out of professional duty or just out of compassion for another human, teachers save lives every day.

A simple "hello how are you" might seem insignificant but it could mean the world to some student in some school who has nothing else or no one else that would bother to make such a gesture. We can support each other more effectively if we take some time to understand the stories that we all carry with us. We need to communicate more and dig a little bit deeper to gain an understanding.

I may have been "Mr. Football", but I did not get a most valuable player award in high school, and I remember why. Funny how certain events in life stick with you. We were at a party one weekend and had way too much to drink. My friend and I decided that it was time to rip into our teammates at the next practice to light a fire under everyone. An attempt to get everyone on the same page and be more motivated to do better, to play better.

Well, when the time came, I discussed with the defense the concerns I had and the expectations that I had for us as a defense and as a team. On the other side of the field, we could hear my friend screaming his head off at the offense, swearing, kicking the dirt, and going nuts. Well, when it came time to vote for the most valuable player his rant stood out much more than the sensible discussion I had with the defense, so as it goes, he won.

What seemed so important during that time means nothing now. I know I was upset but now its more like oh well, no big deal. By the way, our defense played amazing the rest of the year and our offense was nothing more than average. You do not always have to yell to get your point across.

Another interesting point to make here is my friend was very smart and could have gone to university, but he chose not to, and I am not sure why. He was an academic student who did not go, and I was a marginal student who barely passed high school but did go despite all the obstacles.

Interesting, as an educator to gain an understanding from this. Not all academic students want to go to university, and not all marginal students are destined for the lower-paying jobs or laborious types of employment that are accessible to marginal students.

I remember some of the academic students playing around with me and making comments like "the only way you will make it to university is by pushing a broom as a janitor". Ha, ha, funny stuff. At the time they were right.

All the evidence showed I was not an academic student, and I was not headed for university. Instead, my focus continued to be on football. Even though I knew I was not going to university, and I knew I did not have any of the required courses to get in, I went to the University of Alberta spring camp.

This stands out for me because I remember, being young and healthy and being exceptionally good. Good enough for coaches to follow up with me to make sure I had all my applications in order and courses submitted for approval.

Of course, I did not and would not for many more years. I was 17 at the time and would not officially get into university until I was 24. Wow, that seems very strange to think about that now.

I talk a lot about evidence. Looking at the most recent evidence in your life as truth. Your most recent evidence is your truth. When I was 17 my evidence indicated that I was not going to university anytime soon. Your evidence in your life is your truth. **What is your most recent evidence telling you? What will you do differently to change that evidence?**

The next step for me was the Prairie Junior Football League. This was a team made up of the best of the best from high school. All the "MVP" type high school football players assembled into one awesome football team, ages 17-22.

Oddly enough I did not go the year after high school. My high school coach could not believe it. He was literally beside himself with disbelief. I remember him saying "you have your whole life to work, why on earth would you pass up this opportunity, players that take a year off never go back". I remember that talk like it was yesterday and I use it when speaking with student athletes today. My coaches from high school were amazing and had a very heavy influence on me but I did not always listen.

At the time I had a landscaping job that for some reason took priority. I have no idea why. I was the leading tackler on our team, had coaches calling me to come to play and I turned it all down to landscape yards. A real bone head move.

Two things come to mind about this decision. Number one: If I would have had some parental guidance along the way I might have made better decisions, but I did have "parental guidance" in the form of my coaches and I refused to listen and secondly, learning how to listen is a skill we all need to learn and do a better job of, and I thought as an adolescent that I knew better.

Adolescents do not know better; they need guidance and support to help them. I know I have said this before, but it is an important point. We assume our children are independent and ready to make their own decisions, but children are too young. Twelve-year-old children are not independent just because they can walk from the bus to the house and punch in a code to get in their homes.

We pull away far too soon and this has damaging effects on our youth. They develop anxiety, insecurities, and the uncertainty of their decision-making abilities can have lifelong, lingering effects.

Ever meet someone indecisive, could not make a decision to save their lives? I believe a lot of this is a product of their past, their childhoods. We are all shaped by our environments, and our observations of others. It defines who we are and who we may become. However, and I will discuss this in greater detail later, we all have choices we can make.

Try and resolve issues from our past and move on or be a victim of our past experiences and continually blame others for our issues and problems. Passive-aggressive tendencies come to mind but as I said I will discuss these issues in more detail later.

Adults need to be more accountable for the children they are responsible for. As a teacher and as a parent we need to keep fighting the good fight. Of course, it is easier to throw your hands up in the air and give up. Some of you give up without even knowing it. Some teachers see misguided students and label them as "troublemakers" or "not interested in learning".

"Do not let the busyness of life be your excuse for not parenting your child. We are all busy, there is no excuse."

Some parents believe they have inherited a "bad seed", or comment that "there's nothing this kid will respond to". We need to look deeper than this. We are what we are for a reason. If a student is labeled as "not interested in learning" that student will not be interested in learning. You will not teach them, and they will not learn.

We need to find ways to reach all our students not just the ones that are interested in learning because let us face it, if you are 100% honest with yourself, you would admit that you went through a phase of not being interested in learning and hopefully no one gave up on you. If we give up on our students, we teach them that people do not care.

Parents also need to wake up and get involved. No one cares that you are working full time, and overtime and running around doing different activities. Do not let the busyness of life be your excuse for not parenting your child. We are all busy, there is no excuse.

Remember I said you can pay now or pay later. This point is important so I will say it again. Cutting corners now will make life a lot worse later. It is easier to guide a child than an adolescent, but we wait too long and try to shape and mold our teens, but it is too late. Here is the problem I see often.

Children reach the age of 10 or 12 and parents start to experience some of the benefits of independence because their children are a little more equipped to manage themselves. In other words, stay alive while you run out to the store for milk. This is not the problem.

The problem is it starts just running to the store for milk but becomes much more way too soon. Next thing you know they are staying home alone more often and for longer periods. They begin making meals and lunches for school. We as parents back away too soon.

Do not let a child's ability to survive at home alone fool you into thinking they are independent enough to make good decisions. They need you more than ever at this age and many parents make the mistake of letting go when they really should be holding on.

Here is the last phase of my football career and then we will focus more on the next phase of my journey and additional strategies that you can use in your life. My football journey did not end when I took a year off to landscape yards, as my coach predicted. I was determined to play again so I did.

Before the next football season, I began to get ready. I had lost about 30 lbs., and no one could understand what happened and there was a serious illness in the news at that time and all my friends knew about this serious illness was you lost a lot of weight. So naturally, being adolescents, they thought I had this serious illness and was extremely sick. I did not have it; I was out of the gym for a year and lost all the muscle from the previous years of working out.

As I have mentioned before, my healthy distraction, my single focus was on working out. Lifting weights and running. When I played in high school, I played at about 210 lbs., big for a 5' 8" young man. I worked out every day and discovered that I was stronger than just about everyone, but it would take more than this to be successful in coming back.

Being out of the game for a year hurt me more than I could ever have imagined. All those coaches that went out of their way to talk to me were now upset I took a year off and showed up to camp 30 pounds lighter.

Playing for the Edmonton Wildcats ended up being a complete bust, at least that is what I thought at the time, but as you will see life takes a lot of interesting turns before we arrive where we are supposed to arrive. I had the talent but not the support and to be completely honest I spent a lot of time drinking and partying, which was a huge distraction and if I could change that part of my life, I would, in a heartbeat.

Poor choices, but I was old enough now to know better but did not do what I needed to do. It is one thing to be aware that you need to make changes and it is another thing to make the adjustments necessary to make things better. Remember, awareness is important but a willingness to make adjustments is even more important.

The Wildcats never started me consistently in the three years I played there. This was unbelievable, to my ego, but now that I look back, I have a better understanding of why. It was like my lack of success in hockey. The Edmonton Wildcats were, and still are a very good organization but there is only so much an organization can do when players are not focused on the right things at the right time.

This was a time in my life when I was not making good choices, I was not putting in the time and effort necessary to be successful. I could not keep thinking it was because I was not supported, guided, and encouraged. I was now old enough to know better but did not do what I needed to do.

I often believed that I needed a push to be more motivated and driven but now I understand that sometimes it needs to come from within and I needed to lean on my evidence from my high school years as my evidence that things could be okay. I have mentioned throughout this book the importance of living and learning from the past and doing a better job moving forward. What I learned from the Wildcats would help me with the next phase of my life, at least the football part.

When my days with the Wildcats were over, I knew in my heart that I could have achieved much more, and I wanted to prove this to myself. I could not go on with this heavy feeling of being a failure in the sport I loved and in a sport that gave so much to me.

I had to do something, and I had to do it quickly before another year of playing football was lost due to my lack effort to make it happen. I went to the University of Alberta to talk to the head coach there. His name was Coach Jim Donlevy. He had been there for years. He said you have a couple of choices. One, you can upgrade and come play for us, or two, you can go to the U.S. and play for a junior college team for a couple of years and hopefully get on with a bigger school after that.

This was great advice from a well-respected coach in the football community. I had no idea at the time, but this coaches' advice changed my life in so many ways I cannot imagine where I would be if I headed down a different path. Again, someone in my life that cared enough to share their wisdom with me.

If you remember, I was the worst student ever so upgrading was far down on my list of achievable goals and at that time in my life I did not believe in my self enough to think upgrading was the way to go. In my mind the logical solution to this problem was to make a highlight reel of my playing days with the M.E. LaZerte Voyageurs and the Edmonton Wildcats with the plan to send it to different colleges in the U.S. and see if anyone was interested.

It turned out good but looking back I can recognize that I took a real beating while playing for the Wildcats, so a few lingering injuries were also something I needed to be aware of as I shifted my focus forward on this next adventure. I sent this highlight reel out to a few schools and believe it or not there were a few interested in me coming down for a visit.

First stop, why not Minot (Minot, North Dakota). That was the joke at the time, why not Minot. It was actually a nice place and a very well-run program. I drove down with a couple of friends to visit the campus. There were no guarantees here. We had to pay, and we had to make it all happen on our own. I had no money, so this was not an option for me. Looking back, I now get a better sense of how poor we were. Remember my mother worked a low paying job her whole life and continued to struggle financially at this time.

This whole idea of going to university to play football was a stretch at best. No money, no required courses completed to get into university and no real guidance to show me how to make this happen. I had to focus on my journey and do what would be best for me moving forward.

My friend made the team in Minot and played there a couple of years. I was happy to see him find success there. I had another offer, and it was a big one. Montana State Wildcats. I was invited to come down as a walk on. If it went well, I could get a scholarship to play there. I used to question myself over this decision, the decision not to go but, who was I kidding, this was not the path for me.

As you can imagine there was not a high demand for 5' 8" linebackers on a U.S. College football team and as I had mentioned earlier, I took a beating playing for the Edmonton Wildcats. Physically I was banged up and recovering, and to be honest there may not have been enough tape in the trainer's bag to hold me together on a team of much larger men on a U.S. College football team.

I decided to stay home and upgrade so I could go to the University of Alberta. I know this may seem like a crazy, unrealistic decision to make as you will recall I was a horrible student, but I was determined to play again and end my football career my way.

THE MIDDLE YEARS

As crazy as taking a year off between high school football and prairie junior football, I was now taking a year and a half off to upgrade before trying out for the University of Alberta Golden Bears. You will remember the last time I was there at a spring camp I was 17. This was against all odds but seemed to follow the script from my past of enduring and navigating the challenges in front of me.

A 5' 8" linebacker who just got knocked around in the prairie junior league for 3 years is going to upgrade and play for the Golden Bears Football Team. Remember I was the worst student ever. Another moment in my life that some guidance would have come in handy or maybe not.

Remember there are people in our lives that due to their dysfunction and negative view of the world would not hesitate to discourage us from pursuing a dream. I will discuss the value of your inner circle people later.

Perhaps it was good no one was around to talk me out of upgrading and doing more with my life at that time. I think that the discussion would have probably been more about going into the trades and starting a life without football rather than upgrade and going back to play more football.

Do not ever give up on a dream. Put in the time and effort and pay attention to your evidence. If you have evidence of an effort and evidence that it is possible then keep moving forward. I often think of the old song "Dreams never die just the dreamer". Stay focused forward on better days ahead and do not give up on something that is important to you.

I applied to Concordia College in Edmonton, Alberta. They had an upgrading program called the University and College Entrance Program (U.C.E.P). I had been out of school now since I was 17.

I was now 22 and could no longer play football unless I took this next step. I remember the counselor giving me the old pep talk saying, "you have the world by the tail", "you can achieve anything you set your mind to". All I wanted to do was pass the English and Biology so I could meet the requirements to get into university so I could play football. World by the tail, what did that mean? This was not going to be easy.

On a side note, to help build a better understanding, I was going to enter university as a mature student and at that time the mature student eligible age was 24 and instead of needing 5 academic courses from high school, I only needed 3.

> *"...give someone some hope and it's amazing what they can do."*

As I have mentioned throughout, I was not a good student, and this was more challenging than anything I ever did in the past, but I remember my teachers never gave up on me despite my lack of efforts so perhaps there was some hope. It is amazing what happens when you are motivated, and you have a goal to work towards.

I often tell my clients this. Create a big picture, something you can work towards, and something to motivate and drive you to keep you focused and on track. Creating a vision board is an effective strategy. **What would you put on your vision board?**

My big picture was football and football would have been the only thing on my vision board. I was motivated and driven (probably, with regards to academics, for the first time in my life) to get this done so I could play football.

Perhaps all the setbacks from my life were now going to be what drove me to succeed. I believe that everything, the good, the bad and the ugly, happens for a reason. As hard as it was and as lonely as it often was, I believe I needed to go through what I went through to arrive where I arrived.

Bottom line, after one year of upgrading I passed my coursework and now had the requirements necessary to get into the University of Alberta as a mature student. Yes, 24 years old and starting university. Now at the spring camp when the coaches asked if I had my application and coursework all submitted, I could say, "yes sir, all done".

Obviously, this was not the easy way to go. I have discovered throughout my life that I tend to take the more difficult road. The friends I had in high school had already graduated university and here I was just starting.

I remember not caring because I was on a mission to play football again. Nothing was going to stop me. Nothing would distract me from getting on a team and playing again. I was also working out hard throughout this time away from the game. Back working out, back to a respectable weight, somewhere around 215 lbs. I was also running every day so all the pieces of the puzzle for this comeback were falling into place. This all took time and effort.

If you are willing to put in the time and effort there is nothing you cannot accomplish. This was my story to write, and no one else from this point forward was going to decide how it would played out. Remember we do not have to live within someone else's script. Write your own story. Make it what you want it to be.

The upcoming spring camp was going to be the most intense week I would have had in a long time. I had not played a game or participated in a practice for 2 years. I had a lot to prove. I was determined to overcome all the obstacles to become the starting middle linebacker for the Golden Bears. Spring camp would be very physically and mentally demanding as we only had a week to make an impression on the coaches and hope we did enough for them to call us back for the main camp in the fall.

I mentioned getting knocked around a lot in the junior prairie league and I also had a lot of injuries. The one that seemed to always surface at the worst of times was a pulled hamstring injury and of course this happened again halfway through spring camp.

I was disappointed but reframed it in a way that helped me stay positive. I looked at my evidence. I had a good few days of spring camp and did not look out of place. I was also thankful that this injury occurred during spring camp rather than during the main camp in the fall. Reframing is an effective strategy. Shift your focus from the negative and onto the positive. Again, focus forward on better days ahead, using your evidence that it will be okay.

Tom Wilkinson was the head coach. Coach Wilkinson is a hall of fame quarterback from the Canadian Football League (CFL). He was not your typical prototype professional football player. Anyone that knows him would agree. Anyone that knows him would also agree that he was not only an amazing football player but an amazing human being.

We related well to each other. Probably because in sports and in life we most likely achieved more than most would have predicted. I remember one time as I was recovering from a shoulder injury, he saw me and said not to worry. He said you have done so much and will be back soon; you are an overachiever.

At the time I was not sure what that meant but now understand what he was trying to say. Despite the obstacles I continued to navigate through the challenges to find success. I achieved more success than was expected. There were a couple other occasions where Coach Wilkinson went above and beyond to help me achieve success. At that time in my life, I would not have made it without his support.

My unit coach was Pete Lavorato, a defensive back from the CFL. He was a great coach, one of the best I ever had. He knew the game inside and out and could really communicate well and teach us strategies, techniques, and most importantly how to break down game film.

There was a time with the Golden Bears when all the unit coaches were ex-Edmonton Eskimos football players. Amazing now thinking about being on the field and being coached by my childhood heroes. The Edmonton Eskimos were arguably one of the greatest dynasties in professional sports.

Coaching would not be the issue in my comeback, the other linebackers were the issue. I made the team, there was never any doubt in my mind this would happen, but this was University football, and everyone was much bigger, like 6' 4" linebackers, not 5' 8" linebackers. I worked hard and did what I was told.

I was not necessarily faster than the others, but I was quicker. Some might not understand this part. Someone can run 40 yards fast, but it may take them some time to build up the speed. I was quick. Short distances like 10 to 20 yards. I also studied film more than anyone else. Studied film more than anyone else. I repeat that because studying was never a part of who I was but give someone some hope and it is amazing what they can do.

I was motivated and driven to succeed and if studying film was what I had to do to gain an edge I was going to do it. I did not have to have a history of success in academics or lean on the support and guidance of others to get this done. This was something I could do, on my own and now as I reflect, I guess a lot of what I did was on my own. Live and learn from your past and do a better job moving forward.

The linebackers ahead of me were all on route to tryouts for the CFL so I had to be patient. About two or three games into the season the starting middle linebacker went down with a knee injury, and I was up and ready to go. I started 3 games in a row and played pretty darn good. As we neared the end of the season the injury to the old starter had healed and he was ready to take back his spot, which Lavorato gave back without hesitation.

Back then fifth-year players had all the power and the fact that this was his last game, in his last year of university football made the decision easy for Lavorato. So Lavorato gave me the news. I was pissed off, to say the least. I remember telling Lavorato that "this was fucking bullshit and he could go fuck himself". Tip here for all the players out there, you do not ever say those words to a coach that is the one that decides who plays.

Reflecting on this time I am embarrassed that I said what I said. To my credit I did apologize at the end of the year, Lavorato was great about it, he said he understood and looked forward to the next year. I looked forward to next year as well. I was extremely optimistic about my second year. The fifth-year linebackers had moved on and I had a good first year of playing and learning so I felt confident and hopeful.

As luck would have it, and if you have been paying attention to the obstacles that always seemed to surface for me, you could probably guess what happened next. Coach Lavorato was not back for the following season. This could potentially be another setback for me. I just finished proving myself to the coach and was next in line to start but now we had a new coach, and I would have to start all over again.

You never know what life is going to throw at you but if we lean on our evidence from the past, the good and the positive evidence from the past, we learn that it will be okay. Remember we touched on using evidence from the past to dispute negativity in your life. I would use my evidence from the past that it would be okay. **What evidence can you bring forward to help you dispute negativity you are faced with today?**

The new coach and defensive coordinator would be an ex-golden bear linebacker, and from all reports from others who were familiar with him, he was 'one tough son of a bitch' that would tear you a new one if you stepped out of line.

I remember one time at practice we were walking through our blitz package and one of the guys stepped through the wrong hole. You would have thought he committed a murder. Coach Morris ripped into him like I never witnessed before. This guy was no longer a starter.

We were taught that mistakes could cost us a game and there was no room for errors in a game like football. Football is one of those unique games, the ultimate team sport. It is broken down into 3 teams within one. You have the offense, the defense, and the special teams. All three parts needed to work together to achieve the goal of winning and being successful.

There was lots of pressure on me. I was the middle linebacker, the quarterback of the defense. I called the plays in the huddle, I called the formations when the offense came out, and generally made sure everyone was lined up and ready to go.

I also felt pressure because I did not want to let my teammates down let alone myself. The Prairie Junior League almost killed me mentally and physically and this was my last chance to prove to everyone, including myself that I belonged.

Looking back, being on a team and having coaches and player around really saved me. We all need someone; we all need something to keep us going. **Who do you have in your life and what do you have in your life that keeps you going?**

This should have been the happiest time of my life, but I did not have anyone to share it with. My mother was around but not around. I saw her during certain holidays like Christmas and Thanksgiving but that was about it.

My stepfather was still kind of in the picture but as I mentioned before he was not a communicator. I remember driving out, as a young boy, to his cabin at Garner Lake, a two-hour drive, and he would not say more than a word or two to me the whole trip.

To all the parents reading this, please talk to your children. It is so important. I see so many parents and children/adolescents driving around in silence, or the teen has their head down texting. Create some dialogue, say something, anything. Be engaged with your children. This is the most important parenting strategy I can provide you...engage with your children.

> *"We can sit around and hope for things to get better but then we are just sitting around hoping. We need to take initiative, be proactive."*

Once I became the starter for the Golden Bears, I never lost my spot. Every year the team would bring in new linebackers and every year I beat them out and kept my spot. The only time I was out of the lineup was when I was injured. I separated my shoulder probably a dozen times, but I played. The shoulder would heal just enough during the week, and I would play on the weekend.

My motivation for this was the fear of losing my spot in the lineup if I missed a practice or game. This would accurately describe year two and three. My body continued to take a beating, but I kept playing. At that time football was my life. At that time, I did not think or feel like I had anything else.

Finally, I had to have surgery to repair a torn rotator cuff. Interesting part of this story. The team doctor/surgeon had a talk with me before the season and said, "I am not sure how long your shoulder will hold up but when you are ready come find me and we will operate". That is exactly how it played out.

About halfway through my 4th year with the Golden Bears I found my self wandering down the hallways of the University of Alberta Hospital not really knowing where I was going, no appointment, just looking for our team doctor. I do not know how, or why this played out the way it did, but as unlikely as it would be, I found him. We had a brief conversation, he directed me to a reception area to make an appointment to book my surgery.

At the time I did not realize it but as it turned out this would be the end for me, eighteen years of playing football were now over. This was a disappointing time in my life, and it was not just about the injury.

I want to mention something important here as I have discussed time and effort. If you are willing to put in the time and effort there is nothing you cannot accomplish. I would like to add commitment. In the 18 years of playing football, including the two years practicing with no equipment, I never missed a practice, not one. Even after my surgery, I showed up at practice that day to be with the team.

One moment really stands out about that day sitting on the sidelines watching my team practice. One player left the field and came to me, Darcy Park, he gave me a quick pat on the back and jogged back onto the field. Outstanding leadership. This still stands out for me today.

Looking back, I could have done the rehabilitation and the physiotherapy and worked my way back however, I missed a lot of school due to my heavy focus on football and now the surgery, and because of this I fell behind in my coursework and was asked to withdraw from the university. Remember I was not a strong student and any amount of school missed would be the end for me.

This, despite all that I had been through in life, was the worst day of my life. I remember praying to God to make this all better for me, but as I would discover later, God had different plans for me.

Now I did not have football or the friends I had made. Once I left the team it felt like I was never there. My phone stopped ringing, no one came around, and I was alone again. Pretty darn depressing. I do not think I felt this low since high school when I had conflicting thoughts about why I was even here.

Once again, I found myself alone and wondering what I could do to make things better. It is times like this when we really need to shift our focus. Even when the evidence seems to be supporting the negativity we are experiencing, we still need to shift our focus off of the negative and on to something positive.

Back then I was so confused. No guidance, no one that seemed to care, other than coaches and teachers but this was not always enough, I still felt alone. I had to pick myself up and get moving.

We all have choices we need to make, and I had to make one. Sit around and feel sorry for myself and continue to be miserable or finish what I started. We can sit around and hope for things to get better but then we are just sitting around hoping. We need to take initiative, be proactive. I knew playing football was over for me now and I would have to shift my focus off the negative and on to something positive.

Despite my heavy focus on football and lack of effort towards my academics, somehow, I completed most of my degree in education and used this as my "something positive" to focus on. Now it was figuring out how to get back on track.

My situation did not look great. I was out of school, out of football, and out of options. I had no money, no food, and I was living in a horrible basement suite that I could not afford. It never looked so dismal.

At times like this it would be easy to give up and lean on the negative, dysfunctional parts of my past. My parents divorced when I was young. I struggled in school. I made plenty of poor choices along the way. Perhaps this was where I was supposed to land after all. Maybe all those so-called experts were right about children from divorced parents.

This is the pattern of negative thinking that gets us into trouble. I refer to it as the 'spiral into the pool of negativity'. Good time to remember one of the strategies discussed earlier. Pump the breaks on the negativity and look for evidence in your life that it can be or will be okay.

Remember, despite my heavy focus on football and lack of effort towards my academics, somehow, I completed most of my degree in education and could now use this as my "something positive" to focus on or my evidence that things could be or would be okay.

I had to finish what I started. I was in the fourth year of my education degree, and I was not prepared to throw away what I accomplished so far. I did what I did years ago and went back and upgraded so I could get back into school and finish my degree.

I went to Grant MacEwan, a college in Edmonton. I took some courses there, courses that would transfer over and allow me to get back into the University of Alberta. There was another problem. I was not allowed to transfer back directly into the Faculty of Education.

Now what? Well, I went to every faculty on campus until one would take me. As luck would have it a nice lady from Native Studies said she would be happy to give me a second chance. Thank God for her. She was my last hope. Throughout my life I have had the good fortune to benefit from the kindness of others. This was another example of someone in education going above and beyond to help me.

Once I was in school again, I focused on getting my work done. There was no more football or friends to distract me but something big was missing. I could not get over the way my football career ended. It was killing me inside. I had to do something but did not know what to do or who to turn to.

My friend Darryl, ex-golden bear football player, was coaching with the Edmonton Wildcats, my old prairie junior football team. He asked me if I wanted to help because his linebacker coach was moving back to Quebec. I said sure. I had no idea how to coach but I knew the position better than anyone on planet earth, so I was cautiously optimistic.

This saved my life. I was back on track, back in the game, working to pay for school, continuing to pass my course work, and on my way to a Bachelor of Education Degree. This all happened because instead of focusing on my problems I focused on solutions to my problems. Once I recognized what the problem was, the way football ended, I took advantage of an opportunity that presented itself, which helped me get my whole life back on track. Too often doors open, and we walk past them instead of walking through them to see what is there.

> *"Sometimes you must let go of something good to reach for something great."*

As it turned out I was a surprisingly good coach. My linebackers were among the best in Canada and based on this success I was able to recruit many more great athletes. I coached with the Edmonton Wildcats for 4 years and I must say it was awesome. I loved it, and the other coaches were great to be around. Most of them I played university football with, so it was like being back with family. I miss that part of my life but sometimes you must let go of something good to reach for something great.

Letting go of the disappointment of not playing football or football not ending the way I would have hoped allowed me to embrace an opportunity that coaching gave me. This is another example of learning from the past and doing a better job moving forward. Let the past fall away and embrace where you are and where you are headed. Do not live life in the past lane. **What can you let fall away so you can better embrace where you are or where you are headed?**

I have mentioned defining moments that we need to reflect on. This time of my life almost seemed like another defining moment. Another obstacle to conquer was not too far ahead. I was a horrible student but managed to get a bachelor's degree in education. Now the challenge would be getting a job in education.

I mentioned when playing football ended many friendships ended as well but as I would discover I was wrong. The relationships you form when being a part of a team are lifelong. I honestly had no idea about this until many years later.

I needed a way into education, I needed someone who was already in education to find me away in. One of my best friends from the Golden Bears' Barclay Spady was the one that opened the door for me. He provided me with contacts and guidance to get my foot in the door. From there it was the kindness of others that helped me find my way. I was a substitute teacher for a few months then a different opportunity presented itself that would once again change my path.

After four years coaching with the Edmonton Wildcats, and now a few months working as a substitute teacher, we had an opportunity to transfer to Norman Wells in the Northwest Territories. This would be an opportunity to make a lot of money in a short time so we could finally afford a house. I had to make the difficult decision to quit coaching with the Wildcats and packed up our duplex and focus forward on our next adventure.

Now for those of you who do not know where Normal Wells is, it is in the northern regions of the Northwest Territories. It is farther north than Yellowknife. It is cold, and dark in the wintertime and hot, and sunny in the summertime. The bugs were huge, the ravens were huge (they would steal bags of groceries from the back of pick-up trucks). Norman Wells was a fly in fly out community. No roads in or out other then a winter road that was open for a short period of time in the dead of winter. I loved my time there, it was awesome. Maybe it was the isolation that I enjoyed or just being somewhere new and different but overall a great experience.

I graduated from the University of Alberta, had been a substitute teacher, and was now eager to find a job at the local school in Normal Wells. I did not have a lot of teaching experience other than as a substitute teacher for a few of months. I did however have coaching, which helped me become a more confident, competent teacher.

I was about to embark on a dream, a dream I did not even know I had until now. All my life I relied on the kindness of others to get me through, and the teachers and coaches were paramount in this journey and now here I was, I was a teacher, ready to teach.

I already knew how I was going to be. I was going to be the teacher that gave kids a break. I was the student that no one wanted and now I could be the teacher that embraced the misfits and provide hope for the students so they would understand there is a legitimate chance for them to pursue their dreams and succeed.

All it takes is a couple of adults who care to make a world of difference. I remember countless times I would hope and pray for a break and sometimes it came and sometimes it did not. I came to appreciate when a break was appropriate and when it was not. I get it. You put in an effort, a real effort, and still fall short, you deserve a break. You put in little to no effort, and you do not get a break. That is life. I have discovered that a willingness to put in time and effort is a formula for success.

Well, the excitement of Norman Wells ended quickly. The job I was promised disappeared. My first of many brushes with the politics of education. Apparently when you graduate with a "teacher's certificate" you are more qualified than a Bachelor of Education graduate from the University of Alberta.

Obviously, this is not true but the principal at that time was hiring her hometown people. So, there I was in Normal Wells not as a full-time teacher but instead just hoping to be a substitute teacher as often as possible. The only other competition around was the janitor. Yes, that is right. Sometimes the janitor would dress up nice and fill in as a substitute teacher. You may think this is unbelievable, unheard of, but it is the truth. When you live in a small town you do things differently than the big city.

I did eventually work consistently, had a great time with the students, and appreciated the opportunities I was given. I was what I wanted to be, the teacher that gave students a break if they earned it. I was fortunate enough to teach elementary-age children. It was a lot of fun. Very demanding but a lot of fun. I honestly believe enjoying your job is key. Find something you love, something you have a passion for, and make it happen.

If you are going to a job just for the money, for the health benefits, for the pension and not because you want to be there, you will not be happy. You will be miserable, and this will follow you home. Be careful. Remember the most important place is your home, and the most important people are in your home. Do not bring negativity home with you.

We were supposed to spend five years in Norman Wells but ended up leaving after one and a half years. It was a blessing in disguise. It was tough to fit into a community that was not very welcoming of "people from the south". Returning to Sherwood Park, Alberta and settling into the next phase of our lives would end up being a great, next landing spot.

Once the children were old enough, we enrolled them in school and their journey into the world of learning would begin. As I have previously mentioned, the teachers I have had the privilege of working with and the teachers that worked with our children, were amazing.

They cared for them, they nurtured them, and they understood them. What more could you ask for and if that were not enough, they taught them Math, Science, English, and Social Studies. They taught them how to interact appropriately, and they taught them how to be a team player. I know I have said this many times, but teachers are awesome, and we never really appreciate them as much as we should.

> "If you are too busy to participate in the lives of others, you are simply too busy."

I often talk about perspective and taking a step back to see the big picture. Peeking over the fence, looking down the street to see what is down the road instead of sitting stuck in the here and now. Today we are simply too busy and too focused on the wrong things. Our priorities are all messed up. In today's fast paced world, being ahead of the game means nothing more than being on time. We have pushed life so far; we are racing but losing. Racing around to do this and to do that, pushing life so hard that we are not living at all. We are merely racing around trying to complete tasks we have scheduled ourselves to do. What we need nowadays is perspective and that's exactly what teachers can provide.

Gaining perspective allows us to slow down, take a step back and look at the big picture. It gives us an appreciation for what is important. I know we are all busy and we all have serious commitments we need to attend to. However, making connections with the people in our lives, engaging with our spouses and children, and helping others when we can, should all be items at the top of our lists. Like I said before, if you are too busy to participate in the lives of others, you are simply too busy.

It seemed up to this point that my life was always busy. Always chasing the next thing. Always too busy to participate in the lives of others. I was in the trap that I talk about so much with my clients. We fall into the trap of "once I get there it will all be better". Once I get that new job life will be great. Once we can afford that house life will be great. Once we have that vacation life will be great. Always focused on the next thing. Always relying on the next thing to make us happy.

We need to be happy with who we are, how we are and more specific to this part of our discussion, where we are. We cannot just keep chasing the next best thing. Embrace where you are whether it is a temporary parking spot or your final landing spot. Appreciate it for what it is.

There will be ups and downs in life. There will be times when our plans get changed. I believe everything happens for a reason. We must work hard to be aware of what is going on around us and be willing to make adjustments along the way. I often talk about my teachers because they were a big part of my journey and a big part of my successes.

From an early age, as you have read already, my teachers gave me opportunities I would not have had without them. They were there when no one else was. I remember teachers spending extra time with me, caring about me, providing extra support for me. Some did not know my life story but still were there because that is what teachers do; they care.

The teachers that did know about my life were supportive and offered timely advice and guidance. They certainly did not have to. They were busy teaching; they did not have to be guardians as well, but they were. Junior High could have been an official gong show but as I mentioned sports kept me away from drugs and teachers kept me accountable, so my behaviors did not go too far off the rails.

I remember the band teacher made the biggest impact on me and I hope you can appreciate and recognize that teachers who teach option classes have great value. School is not just about Math, Science, English, and Social Studies. It is about learning how to be a good, productive citizen in today's society. It is also about learning how to cooperate, collaborate, and have a positive impact on others.

Back to the impact my band teacher had on me. I had the worst acne ever. I was so embarrassed to be seen but my band teacher helped me. One day in the middle of class he asked to see him in the hallway. He said, "listen, don't worry about your appearance right now, in time the acne will go away." He said, "who knows maybe one day you will be a model." He did not have to do this. He had a classroom full of students, but he took the time to talk to me and make my life a little better.

I am 53 years old, and I remember this as a major, defining moment in my life. It was not a professional hockey player or a professional football player, it was a teacher. A teacher who went above and beyond the call of duty to change my life. Little things lead to bigger things. Life is a series of small steps that take us to better places if we make appropriate choices along the way. A small gesture made a big difference in my life and made junior high a bit more tolerable.

High School was similar with regards to the support of teachers and now coaches would also play an important role in guiding me. Teachers and coaches helped keep me on track and focused forward on what could be instead of focusing on what was. There always seemed to be someone watching out for me.

As I mentioned earlier, I was not a good student at all, and high school was often a struggle for me, but teachers and coaches recognized this early on and seemed to shift their focus in order to support me in a better way. Many knew my background, and many contributed to helping me focus on what could be rather than on what was. **Are you focused too much on the past and on what should have been or are you learning to focus forward on better days ahead?**

Now continuing with my journey as an adult now entering the world of education as a profession. Norman Wells was not everything we had hoped it would be and we needed to make an adjustment and change our path once again.

We made our return and landed in Sherwood Park, Alberta in hopes of buying a house, settling down and finding my next job in education. Again, my friend Barclay would play an important role in my journey moving forward. He helped me connect with the right people and helped me find a full-time teaching job at Bev Facey High School and also pulled me back into coaching football.

This opportunity would not have been possible if the principal at the time, Bev Fleming, had not been kind enough to provide me a chance at a time when it was difficult to find opportunities in education.

Still being early on in my career as an educator I had a lot to learn and was fortunate enough to work for one of the best in the business. Landing here with Bev Fleming and her team of administrators, counselors and teachers was the best possible place I could have landed.

As children, adolescents, and adults, we are lifelong learners. Going to school to learn is one thing but learning from others who are doing the job provided so much more for me. Of course, it takes a willingness to listen and learn. Some struggle with this. For example, some get out of school, and they think they already know everything. As we get older we start to understand that we can benefit and learn from the experiences of others.

I would need to lean on the experiences of others as I was now teaching computers and psychology. I did not have a lot of experience at that time in either subject but again, leaning on the experience of others helped me get through my first year. This was a major accomplishment on a couple fronts. First, it was my first full year of teaching and I loved it. Second, it was the beginning of my victory over anxiety. The school in Norman Wells had 158 students from K to 12. Bev Facey had 1200 students from grade 10 to grade 12. Overwhelming to say the least.

I have often talked about thought life throughout this book. Thoughts influence our feelings, emotions, and behaviors. If negative thoughts take over, we potentially could spiral into a pool of negativity. Anxiety is the overthinking and over analyzing of events from the past, present or future. I was in an environment that was overwhelming, and I was overthinking and over analyzing every moment of every day.

My strategy to overcome this was shifting my thoughts from the negative to the positive. Finding a healthy distraction to refocus my attention. Instead of focusing on the crowded hallways and letting this anxiety of being around so many people stop me in my tracks, I used the power of thoughts to overcome this.

It was as simple as singing a song in my head. This was my distraction. I even remember the song. It was the song from the Beatles, "When I'm Sixty-Four". Odd, I know, but it was the song I had my grade 4 class perform at the school in Norman Wells. For some reason it was stuck in my head and was the song that helped me overcome the anxiety I was experiencing in a school with 1200 students.

I have used this strategy with clients as well, but I call it the "everything will be okay song". You know that song we all have that comes on the radio and it changes our mood. That song that every time we hear it, we feel better. Music is a powerful tool. **What is your everything will be okay song?**

Now I am not suggesting that this is the solution to all our problems. I am using this as an example to demonstrate how little tweaks and adjustments in our daily routine can make the day better for us. Remember, awareness and a willingness to make adjustments.

With the teaching part of this experience well under way there was the other part of this puzzle still to be explored. I was a bit hesitant to coach high school football and had to work hard at not viewing this as a step down from my previous experiences coaching with the Edmonton Wildcats. Despite this hesitation, this was, by far, the most rewarding experience coaching I had ever had.

I would be the defensive coordinator for the Bev Facey Falcons. Proud to be able to say that. The young men we coached were outstanding and their parents were amazing. I really admired how committed the parents were. They came to all the games and some even came to the practices.

This is something I never experienced growing up. As I mentioned before my mother/parents came to two games in eighteen years so to see parents be so involved was great even though at times it made me feel sad that I did not have the same support growing up.

As I mentioned earlier, and staying true to the theme of this book, we do not want to focus too much on what should have been and should always work hard to focus forward on better days ahead, but we are all human and we will all have these moments when we wonder "what if".

Again, instead of focusing on what should have been I embraced and appreciated what I was seeing from the parents as they supported their children. As I mentioned before, a great group to work with.

So great, if fact, we won a Provincial Tier One Championship in 2002. I can say with all honesty that the team the year before was probably better, but this team was a group of young men who were determined to play as a team and make sacrifices for each other.

We had a shared vision. A shared vision moving forward. This is a concept I use with couples and families. Sit down with your partner or sit down as a family and talk about your shared vision moving forward. Your family is like a team. **What are your hopes, dreams, and expectations for the story you are writing?**

So, at this point in the story the assumption may be that I have this new teaching position, have returned to coaching football, and all is well. I thought so too however, staying true to my story and my journey there would be another potential setback.

The end of the year was approaching and there were many discussions about staffing and budgets. This was the time of year when some teachers would get let go due to the budget the principal had to work with. There are a lot of moving parts to this. Enrollment was a big part of how schools were funded and if enrollment went down the budget went down so some teachers were moved. I was new, in my first year there and I was teaching computers and psychology. I was let go, surplused.

As I have said before, I believe everything happens for a reason. Remember I mentioned Bev Fleming the principal of Bev Facey. This was a difficult decision for her, but she did something amazing for me. She reached out to a colleague of hers and put in a good word and arranged for me to have an interview with him. This gesture was over and above anything I would have expected. I am so grateful for her kindness.

As it turned out, the interview went well and following true to my belief that everything happens for a reason, I was now moving from a high school to a junior high school. I embraced this as a new opportunity. I moved from Bev Facey High School to Sherwood Heights Junior High and as luck would have it, I was able to continue coaching football at Bev Facey so in my world everything was great.

The principal was Frank Belyea. He was another great administrator that I was really blessed to work for. He saw the value in me continuing to coach football and was supportive in allowing me to do so. He was also supportive helping me grow as a young teacher. I was able to teach computers and now also had the opportunity to teach Physical Education. I was one of the gym teachers. In my mind at this time there was nothing more I needed. I was teaching Phys. Ed. and computers and coaching football. Life was good.

I mentioned before how I got stuck in a trap. Always chasing the next thing. Never really feeling settled. I was now in a place where I had achieved everything I had set out to achieve yet something was missing. Something was still missing. How was this possible? I have had many male clients who have described this scenario to me. They went to school, graduated from university, found a great job, have a wife and children, were able to engage in activities that they were interested in and yet they were not happy. Nothing made them happy, and they could not figure out what was missing. I know now that this is depression. If you have everything but cannot enjoy what you have, you may be depressed.

We discussed my anxiety a little bit so far and now depression. Anxiety and depression are usually linked in some way. When we are anxious we withdraw, isolate, and find ourselves alone in a place we have created that makes us feel safe. This safe place also makes us feel alone and isolated, which leads us to feeling lonely and depressed.

When discussing anxiety and depression we want to explore our thought life. In other words, thinking about thinking. What are you thinking about? Are you consumed with negativity despite, from the outside, looking in, appear to have everything anyone could ever want?

Clients with depression present with this all the time. From the outside, looking in, there life looks amazing, but it is not. Remember we talked earlier about thought life. Guard your thought life. Do not allow negative, intrusive thoughts to undermine your successes. Despite having everything you think you wanted or thought you needed you are not happy.

I would say you have negative, intrusive, dysfunctional thoughts tripping you up. This is an area that we would explore during our sessions. Remember we want to dispute negativity with evidence it will be okay. Evidence in your life is the truth. The negative, intrusive, dysfunctional thoughts are a lie. Do not buy the lie. Dispute it.

So, as I was discussing earlier, I had a good job, was teaching areas that I really enjoyed, was able to coach football and really seemed to have landed in a great spot. Despite all this, something was missing.

As a teacher in junior high, students would often come to me with some of their issues and concerns and often I felt more like a counselor than a teacher. This led me to talk to the school counselor to ask how I could become a school counselor. Her advice sent me down the path of a master's program to work towards a Master's in Counselling Psychology.

We all may remember at this point that I was the worst student ever. Struggled to graduate high school, struggled to complete a Bachelor of Education degree, and now would dive into a master program.

Now it may not be surprising to learn that the University of Alberta was not interested in having me back to do a master's program. Perhaps this would be the end of my journey. After all I landed in a good place and should be happy where I was. I say to clients if you encounter a wall along your journey you do not stop there.

You go over, under or around it, but you do not stop. I was not sure what to do next and if it were not for the kindness of the school counselor this would be the end of this story. She found a program at City University based out of Bellevue Washington that operated out of Grant MacEwan University.

She put this information into my mailbox in the staffroom. Again, the kindness of others kept hope alive for me. She did not have to do this; she was busy enough trying to manage junior high students and the emotional ups and downs those students at that age experience. She was also involved in helping the administration and teaching classes, so I know she was busy but still took the time to help me.

When I work with clients transitioning from one job to another, leaving one phase of life and entering a new one, I encourage them to pursue something they have a passion for. I am a firm believer that if you are willing to put in the time and effort into something you have a passion for, you can achieve anything.

That sums up my master's degree program. I put in the time and effort and had a passion for learning about how I could help others. Motivated and driven to do for others what others had done for me my whole life. In my final year of the master's program, I was on the Deans List. If you live life in the past you stay there.

If I focused on being a horrible student I would be a horrible student. Instead, I focused on my most recent evidence. We can gather evidence every day to support our efforts and beliefs that it will be okay. As I said before, our evidence is our truth.

When I graduated from City University in 2006 and started the process to become a Registered Psychologist, I was now in my third school. There was an opportunity to be the school counselor at Lamont Junior Senior High School.

Remember part of our previous discussion about he past coming full circle and hitting us in the face. As it turned out, my biological father who passed away at 32 years old of a heart attack, attended Lamont Junior Senior High School. Wild how this all comes full circle.

This school had students from grade 7 to grade 12. I was the school counselor but also taught Psychology, and the Career and Life Management course. I also was the Off Campus Coordinator, which meant I was able to help some of the high school students find jobs and earn credits towards their high school diploma. This also included the Registered Apprenticeship Program helping students find jobs in the trades. Seemed like the perfect fit. I was in a great position to help students achieve success.

As I mentioned I was also in the process of becoming a Registered Psychologist. I was required to put in 1600 hours of counselling services as a Register Provisional Psychologist and was fortunate enough to be able to do most of my hours within my employment with the school board. Other hours I received when I was working with adolescents at a youth centre in Edmonton. This was an interesting place.

Parents who could no longer control their teens would send them here. I will never forget the comment of one of our younger residents. She said, "maybe if more parents took parenting courses before having children there would be less of us in here". Wow, that was quite the statement. She was right. We could all do a better job parenting our children.

Remember awareness and a willingness to make adjustments. If we learn to pay closer attention to our children, our teenagers, and our partners, I believe this awareness will help us make appropriate adjustments to better build and grow positive relationships in our lives.

There was more that needed to be done to complete this part of my journey. All Registered Psychologists in North America need to successfully pass the EPPP exam to become fully registered. This was a 4-hour exam and was well known to be an incredibly challenging examination.

Throughout my life, I have had many challenges to overcome but this was almost more than I could take. 1200 pages of study materials that were broken down into 10 booklets. I also had some audio CD's that I could listen to on my way to work. There was a lot going on at this time in my life.

I was working a full-time job teaching and counselling, I was coaching football, had a young family at home, and continued to struggle with symptoms from several mild, moderate, and severe concussions throughout my days playing football. Reading and remembering was one of those symptoms I struggled with at this time.

As I reflect on this time, I have a better understanding of the value of pursuing something you have a passion for. Just like my passion for football kept me moving forward with my education, my passion for helping others kept me moving forward with this process to be a registered psychologist.

My passion to reach my goal was not without setbacks. I would study one of the booklets until I felt comfortable with the materials and then start the next one but once I was into the next booklet, I would completely forget the last one. It took me several years of studying and a few attempts at the exam to successfully pass the EPPP. Now I had one more hurdle to complete to finish the process of becoming a Registered Psychologist in the Province of Alberta.

Some say this was the easiest part of completing the process, but I was not too sure about that. The last thing I had to do was sit in front of a panel of 3 Registered Psychologists and answer a variety of questions to pass the oral interview part of the examination.

Of course, I was nervous to do this part. When we work hard towards a goal, when we really want something bad enough, we tend to overthink and over analyze every part of it. Anxiety, the unknown and uncertainty of a scenario was something I would have to overcome. It was a challenging hour of questions that I had to answer. This was not easy, but I made it through and would now be able to move forward as a fully Registered Psychologist in the Province of Alberta.

I discuss with my clients the importance of task completion. Work at starting something and finishing something before you move on. Part of this discussion is also about doing as much as we can in one area before we move on to the next.

I do not believe we multi-task. I believe we start a bunch of projects and then become overwhelmed and stressed that we have all these projects on the go with no end in sight. Again, work at task completion. Start something, finish something, move on. This strategy also works well with students or clients who struggle with ADD/ADHD.

Sometimes when we are feeling overwhelmed and stressed and anxious the best thing we can do is focus on one thing at a time. Make a list, prioritize that list, and focus on one item at a time. Start a task, finish a task. As you finish one task at a time you begin to build up some momentum and actually begin to feel good about your accomplishments.

Continuing with my journey. It was in February 2012 that my credentials arrived in the mail. This part of my journey was now complete. I was a fully Registered Psychologist in the Province of Alberta. Now I would have the official credentials and hopefully be more qualified to help and support the students I was working with.

As the story goes you probably could guess this was not going to be the end of my journey. I already had something else in mind and that would be opening my private practice, Greatlife Psychology Centre Inc. At the time I did not fully recognize this as a problem, the fact that I always needed to do more, but rather justified this next move as always something more I had to do or could do.

I talk to my clients about not letting anyone put a ceiling on you. What I mean by this, is do not let someone else determine where you are is where you need to stay. The ceiling is the cap that people put on us. Once we arrive there we have no where else to go. No opportunity to advance your career or achieve more. For me, this is not okay. I believe we need to break through the ceiling and continue to achieve more.

Greatlife Psychology Centre turned out to be the best landing spot of all. Of course, it took and continues to take a lot of professional development, consulting with many colleagues and other helping professionals to stay up to date on the latest techniques and strategies but the opportunities to help others is a dream come true. The Psychologists Association of Alberta

(PAA) and the British Columbia Association of Clinical Counsellors (BCACC) has done an incredible job of providing professional development opportunities over the years.

Now just wanting to have a private practice and being eager to help others did not mean I opened the doors and was busy. It was a slow, tough first year. I used a lot of my savings to keep the doors open. I kept wondering how psychologists grow and build a client base so I did what anyone would do, I googled it. I came across a long list of Employee Assistant Programs (EAP), companies that supported workers in the workplace, which also extended to supporting their families, specifically their children. I signed up for all of them. Soon I was working for over a dozen different EAP's. The referrals started coming in and I was starting to build my client base.

Keep in mind I was still working full time in education, so I worked evenings and weekends at the Greatlife Psychology office. After one year of struggling and a second year of building my client base I was now at a point where I needed to hire someone to take on some of the clients I could not accommodate. As I have said throughout this book, if you are willing to put in the time and effort there is nothing you cannot accomplish.

Soon we had to move from the one room office that we shared. My colleague was there during the day, and I was there in the evenings. I would show up after school around 4 pm and stay there usually until 8 pm. We did this for about a year then found a great spot at the Athabasca Professional Centre in Sherwood Park, AB.

This space allowed for a waiting area, reception desk and three private offices. There was a point in time where we had four Registered Psychologists seeing clients out of that office. Of course, over time people move on and I always encouraged them to do so. I wanted the private practice I created to help others find what they were looking for in their lives. This was not only for the clients but also for my colleagues. Some left to start their families and others opened their own private practices. Again, I was happy to see them pursue their own hopes, dreams, and expectations for their lives.

My therapeutic orientation, the techniques, and strategies I employ are from Cognitive Behavioral Therapy (CBT). This is one of the most universally accepted therapeutic orientation used in therapy today. I believe because there is so much empirical data that supports its success. When we were doing our master's in counselling psychology program, it was a small cohort of 20 that due to a variety of different reasons went down to 16. Through our discussions and or debates about therapeutic techniques and strategies CBT always seemed to be the best fit for me. I often say that CBT is bible based. Some do not see it that way, but I do.

My interpretation of CBT is thoughts, lead to emotions/feelings and these emotions/feeling impact our behaviors. I say my interpretation because others say that our feelings influence our thoughts. In other words, we feel then we think. I do not agree. The bible talks about guarding your thought life (guard your heart). As we think therefore, we are. You probably can relate to this point. Let me give you a few examples for you to consider.

This could potentially be the worst example ever, but it is one I continually use as it seems to be relatable enough that clients get it. You are at work, its sunny, hot and you start to think about when the day will end. As much as you may love your job you are the type of person who works so you can live, not live so you can work.

During your thoughts of going home at the end of the day you start thinking about how nice an ice-cold beer would taste. You think about this all day long. When you get home, you are having ice-cold beer and if you do not have any ice-cold beer at home, you will be sure to pick some up on your way home from work.

My point here is if it is on your mind you are going to do it. We do the things we are thinking about. Probably why the bible talked about guarding your thought life. Do not let negative intrusive thoughts impact you in a negative way and change how you feel and how you behave.

When I work with couples, we discuss how we think about each other when we are not together. I am referring to the time you are apart during the day. If you spent the whole day having negative thoughts about your partner, you can almost guarantee there will be a big fight when you get home.

It is like you are mentally preparing yourself for a fight. This build up of resentment and anger will be overwhelming and once you arrive home there is sure to be a negative, emotionally driven conflict. Your partner gets blindsided by this wave of negative, and emotional dumping.

From the outside looking in you can see how unfair this is. Makes no sense at all to do this to someone you love but we do this all the time because we allow negative, intrusive thoughts to dominate us throughout the day. When we dwell on negativity it changes how we feel and how we behave. **Can you recall a time when you have done this?**

We even do this to ourselves. We allow negative, intrusive thoughts to change our mood, change how our day will go. These thoughts will change just about everything if we let them. This is the key. If we let the thoughts play out, the thoughts will change us. I work with clients to prevent this. You can call it thought stopping or as I say "pump the brakes" on the negative, intrusive thoughts. Stop dwelling on the negative thoughts.

A strategy I use throughout my work with clients is to learn how to focus forward on better days ahead rather than focus on the negative, intrusive thoughts that continue to trip us up. Too often negativity from our past makes us feel sad, withdrawn, and lonely. This effects our self-esteem, self confidence and self worth.

Negative thoughts, and negative people in your life contribute to how you feel about yourself and the world you live in. We have previously asked the question, what can we do differently to make things better? This is an especially important question we can ask ourselves everyday because the fact is, there must be or can be a better way.

The following is an example of strategies I use with my clients to help them answer the question of 'what can I do differently to make things better'. By design, it is repetitive. We want the strategies to be second nature, and automatic (as much as they can be).

So, here we go. At this point, we start to work on our inventory of successes and achievements. The inventory of successes and achievements is like a warehouse of evidence you can use to dispute negativity in your life. Make note of your successes and achievements and use this evidence to dispute the negativity in your life (this may look like a resume but will include successful relationships as well).

Let us break this down a bit more by merging another strategy we have previously discussed. Awareness and a willingness to make adjustments. We first need to identify the problem. Awareness leads to identifying the problem. **What issues, problems or concerns are tripping you up daily?** This is the awareness part. **What can you do differently to make things better?** This is the willingness to make adjustments part.

Awareness, simply stated, is becoming more aware of our surroundings, be present, be in the moment, pay attention. What are we thinking about? This is where we begin to think about what the problems may be.

We mentioned thought life and negative, intrusive thoughts. The way we think about things, or the things we dwell on, affect how we feel, stir up emotions, and affect our behaviors. Thought life, historically has been a problem.

The bible talks about thought life or guarding your heart. We use this term often in our sessions. Guard your thought life. We do what we think about. If you are dwelling on negativity, you will be in a negative space, and do negative things. Proverbs 23:7 For as he thinks in his heart, so is he.

Using strategies from CBT we explore thoughts, feelings, emotions, stumbling blocks or negative, intrusive thoughts that are tripping us up. Helpful tools we have previously discussed are the inventory of successes and achievements and our warehouse of evidence to help us focus forward on better days ahead.

In our sessions we discuss thought life and the impact the irrational/negative thoughts are having on your day-to-day ability to cope and manage. Trying to dial things down and challenge negative thoughts with evidence from your life that it can be okay.

Awareness and a willingness to make adjustments are all about being aware of what is tripping you up (the negative thoughts) and having a willingness to make adjustments. **What will you do differently to make things better for you?**

Now see how this all ties together. We created our inventory of successes and achievements. Store this inventory in our warehouse of evidence. Dispute negative thoughts with evidence it can be okay. Awareness defined as the negativity in your life. Willingness to make adjustments defined as using your evidence to dispute the negativity.

Learning to focus forward is a main theme throughout this book. Using evidence from our inventory of successes and achievements we want to focus forward on better days ahead. **What evidence have you found in your inventory of successes and achievements?**

Some clients use evidence like academics, credentials, positive work experiences, positive relationships with family and friends. Remember, this is the evidence you will use to dispute negativity.

We use the evidence to help you change your focus from negative thoughts or negative experiences to positive thoughts or positive experiences. We refer to this as the shift.

We shift our focus forward on what is working well now, instead of what was not working from our past. We want to focus forward on better days ahead.

Part of the shift is disputing negative thoughts with evidence it will be okay. We are working on shifting the focus from the negative, doom and gloom, to the positive and better days ahead. Seeking out evidence that it can be better than it has been.

We developed our inventory of successes and achievements to find evidence that it can be okay.

We keep this evidence in our warehouse. We use this evidence to help us focus forward.

We shift our focus on what is working well, instead of what is not. Shift, reframe or refocus from the negative to the positive. Using positive self talk is often an effective strategy. Trying to "erase" negativity with evidence it can be okay.

We have made our transition from building our inventory of successes and achievements to using the evidence in our warehouse to focus forward on better days ahead. Using the tools, we are learning to focus forward on better days ahead.

Recap...Build your inventory. Access your warehouse of evidence. Use your evidence to dispute negativity. Focus forward on better days ahead.

These strategies work for a variety of reasons. A lot of this is common sense. Thoughts effect us everyday. The problem is we often do not do anything about them. When I was asked to withdraw from university I had a choice to make. Dwell on the negativity and fall further away from achieving my goals or shift my focus off of the negative and on to the positive.

Remember I used the fact that I had completed most of my education degree and was determined to finish what I had started. We all have something we can embrace to help dig us out or pull us away from the negative thoughts and feelings that are holding us down. **What can you embrace to help you pull yourself up and out of your pool of negativity?**

Collecting evidence along the way is a valuable strategy. We need to pay attention. We need to focus on what is going well rather than what is not. As I have described earlier, the Greatlife Psychology office was finding success due to the time and effort that we all put in to stay focused on our primary goal of helping others. Whenever we would have concerns about our success we would lean on our most recent evidence that it would be okay.

The Greatlife Psychology office was going well but I still had more I wanted to achieve in education. I was a Counselor and now Registered Psychologist. I was able to do psychoeducational assessments to identify issues, problems and concerns related to our students' academics. I would often say the most effective strategy was to identify the problem and then identify and discuss potential solutions to the problem.

Similar to parts of our previous discussions, what can we do differently to better support this student? Be curious about finding solutions to problems. This part of my career in education was going well but as I said there was more I wanted to do.

Earlier I talked about how busy the counselor was, the one that helped me find the masters program. The reason she was so busy was due to the demands made of her by the school system. Counselors and Administrators', due to budget restraints, often had to teach classes as well. This was similar to my situation.

As I mentioned earlier I was the school counselor, the psychology teacher, the career and life management teacher and the off-campus coordinator taking care of work experience and the registered apprenticeship program. As much as I loved all of this it was too much. I wanted to work my way into an administration position. I wanted to be an assistant principal and hopefully someday be a principal of a school.

My rational for this seemed to make sense. I was already doing a lot of counseling work at my Greatlife Psychology office. Working with children and adolescents, helping them cope and manage better with anxiety, stress, depression, and any school related issues that they may have been struggling with.

I wanted my days at school to be different and I wanted to continue to work my way up within education. Many would ask me why I was still in education when I have a private practice I could go to anytime. My response was always the same. I loved working with the students. I loved creating opportunities for students who could not find or see the opportunities that were available for them.

Too often students would give up, get discouraged and this would be the time when we would notice behavioral changes and problems that would surface in and out of the classroom setting. I believed as an administrator, leaning on my experiences as a counselor and psychologist, I could understand students better and help them find their way in my role as an administrator.

I mentioned politics in education when I was in Norman Wells. That would be nothing compared to what I was about to experience now. We all have a story but sometimes we have to update that story. This is what I had to learn as I tried to break into the role as an administrator.

My story, or the one that people in the education world knew was as follows. Rod Woitas is a counselor in the school system who worked hard to become a registered psychologist and now may be focused to heavily on his private practice and not on his career as an educator.

Of course, there is some truth in this story but at the time it was the old story. I was applying for all the administration jobs that were coming up but was not getting any of them. I was not even getting an interview. This was incredibly disappointing and discouraging. I talked to the person in charge of all of this and as I suspected it was all about the story. The old story was the one they were tripping over. I needed to update my story, or I would continue to be stuck where I was.

Too often others are operating based on our old story. If we do not effectively communicate what we need and what that looks like they simply do not know what it is they can do for us. In my case I had to contact the person in charge, first through a professionally written email, then through a call on the phone.

I will not go too far into this part of my journey, as the point I want to make, is to update your story. Update your story so you can get as many people as possible on the same page and focused forward on the path you hope to venture down. Once I delivered the new story I started to get some opportunities. By opportunities I mean at least I started getting some interviews. Eventually, and most likely due to who I knew rather than what I knew, I broke into the world of administration after several years of being on the outside looking in.

I was excited for this opportunity but knew I was being hired as a counselor who carried the role or label of assistant principal. In other words, I was hired to be the counselor of Sherwood Heights Junior High School but was given the title of assistant principal as well. I know that sounds unbelievable, but it was true.

I was the counselor with the title assistant principal, and I was okay with that. Most of my initial duties were as the counselor. There was a lot of work to do as this was a junior high and there were a lot of students struggling emotionally. I was able to do more and more administrative duties once I had the counselor duties organized and moving in the direction I envisioned.

My experiences as a counselor helped me be an administrator that could give consequences for behaviors and explain it in a way that actually supported what the student needed at that time. I called it the 'long road of life' and it went like this.

"This is an opportunity for you to practice appropriate actions and behaviors necessary to be successful in the "real world". It all comes down to choices. The choices you make will dictate whether you will be successful or not. Having a poor attitude and disrespecting people who are trying to help you achieve success is not appropriate behavior. We are willing to help and support you,

but you must meet us halfway. You must do your part as well, which means showing up on time, doing your work, and handing in your work. Again, this is practice for the "real world". When you gain employment, you will be expected to show up on time, work hard, and be productive. We have expectations. We expect our students to show up, be respectful, do their work, hand in their work, and enjoy their school experience. School should be fun. We encourage students to enjoy their time here but remember why you are here. You are here to get an education, so you have a better chance of achieving success when you transition from school and being a student, into the "real world" as a young adult."

My time as an administrator/counselor lasted three years. As I have discussed throughout this book, we need to have awareness and need to be willing to make adjustments when necessary. My 'chasing' the next thing had to come to an end with my awareness that I may be depressed rather than just motivated and driven to achieve more. I remember my defining moment with regards to this.

I was sitting in my office at the school with stacks of papers to deal with. I called them my stations. That is how I organized what I had to do. Well, these stations were becoming bigger and bigger as I was doing less and less. One day I sat looking at the stations and was frozen. Could not move. Could not lift a finger to get going. I believe, through my studies, and also through my work with clients that this is a clear sign of feeling overwhelmed.

When you are overthinking, over analyzing, never happy, unable to complete tasks, stay focused or having struggles remembering what needs to be done, all clear signs its time to step back and assess where you are. Again, awareness, pay attention, and then willingness to make adjustments, the action part of this strategy.

I dug myself out of this by making a list of 5 items. I prioritized this list and then pushed myself to complete the list. One item at a time. As I began to build momentum from the good feeling of completing tasks I eventually chipped away at all the items and completed my work that had to be done.

Another part of this strategy to overcome feeling overwhelmed is to break your day down into blocks of time. This works for stress, anxiety, depression and as we have noted here the feeling of being overwhelmed with life.

Remember the school timetables we were given? Depending on where you went to school the blocks of time may be different, but the idea will be the same. Let us say the blocks of time are one hour long.

Let us start at 8 am. When I am in my 8 am block of time I do not worry about any other block of time. I just focus on my 8 am block of time. If I am thinking about the 2 pm block of time and everything else I need to do up to that block of time I will begin to feel stress, anxiety and be overwhelmed with what my day holds for me.

So, I discuss with my clients the importance of focusing on one block of time, at a time. Try this and assess as you go along to make your day better.

As I said before, I dug out of my feeling overwhelmed, by making a list of 5 items. I prioritized this list and then pushed myself to complete the list. One item at a time, focused on one block of time, at a time. As I began to build up momentum from the good feeling of completing tasks I eventually chipped away at all the items and completed my work that had to be done. However, we need to live and learn from the past and do a better job moving forward. I knew after this past experience, and I will call it my defining moment in education, that it was time to make another change. There are times in our life when we have to assess our situation and make a decision that is best for us.

> *"Assess your life and do what is best for you because when you are in a good place you are better equipped to cope and manage with all the other moving parts in your life."*

I was working from 7:30 am to 4:15 pm at the school then going to the Greatlife Psychology office arriving around 4:30 pm and then wrapping up at the office around 8:30 pm. This was Monday to Friday. I also started working Saturdays and Sundays. Sometimes we are our own worst enemy in the way we schedule ourselves. Blinded by my desire to accommodate my school and my clients I completely overbooked my self.

I had to make a choice, a decision, and this leads to something I have mentioned throughout this book as a strategy. Be aware and be willing to make adjustments. It was time to think about what I could do differently to make things better for me.

As much as I loved education I had to let it go. Remember earlier I talked about sometimes you have to let go of something good to achieve something great. It was time to let go of education after 20 years and focus my attention on my private practice and my career as a psychologist. Assess your life and do what is best for you because when you are in a good place you are better equipped to cope and manage with all the other moving parts in your life.

Just like years earlier I had to let go of playing football and embrace coaching football, now I had to let go of my career in education and embrace my work as a psychologist. Long story short, I packed up my school office during the summer, handed my keys into central office and that was it. The end of one thing would now be the beginning of another.

THE END - YOUR NEW BEGINNING

The strategies I talk about in this book are the same strategies I use with my clients. I give my clients many different strategies to consider, and they use what works best for them. One strategy does not always work for everyone. I believe if you try some of the strategies discussed, make some tweaks and adjustments, are willing to put in the time and effort to get to a better place, that you will be well on your way to a better life.

We should not fear change. Change is okay. We discussed leaning on our evidence that the decisions we are making will be okay. My decision to leave education may have seemed abrupt but really it was not. There was a build up over time and before it became overwhelming again I had to do what I did.

Here is an example I give for a scenario like this. Try and visualize a couple of these items. You have a bag of pebbles and a tin bucket. You start to toss one pebble at a time into the tin bucket. You see them going in, you even hear them as they hit the side of the tin bucket as they fall to the bottom. You see them, you hear them and at first its not a big deal. Pebbles in a bucket. That is, it.

After a while (the build up) the tin bucket starts to fill up. Its heavy and there is not a lot of room left to add more pebbles. Before you fully realize what is going on the pebbles begin to spill over and fall to the floor.

This is how I describe the build up over time. In our lives, just like the pebbles in the bucket, we have this accumulation that occurs over time.

This is the build up. If we do nothing about it we have some version of an emotional eruption, similar to the pebbles in the bucket spilling over. What we need to do is attend to the issues, problems, and concerns before it becomes too overwhelming, and we explode like a volcano erupting.

Just like we see the pebbles going into the tin bucket, if we do not do something about this it will fill up and spill over. Just like we feel and experience the issues, problems, and concerns in our lives, if we do not do something about this, there will be an emotional eruption or emotional breakdown of some kind.

Remember how I described my time in the office, when there was the build up overtime, and I shut down. My awareness of this allowed me to make appropriate adjustments to make things better. This is what we all need to do. Attend to the issues, problems, and concerns before they become overwhelming. If they do become overwhelming we must make an adjustment and do what is best of us. Best case scenario we are attending to the issues, problems, and concerns before they build up and become overwhelming. We do something before the pebbles spill onto the floor.

Let us continue with the strategies discussed so far as well as discuss more of my story as it relates to stress, anxiety and pushing through adversity. Previously I discussed my childhood and adolescence based on how I remembered it but did not discuss it from the viewpoint of a counselor/psychologist.

As I wrote about my early and middle years I highlighted family, football and some of the other supports that were there. I can now look back and describe parts of my experience through the lens of a practicing psychologist.

Through my own experiences and the lived experiences of others I have discovered that dwelling on negative thoughts, stirs up negative feelings and emotions to the point that we become consumed with negativity.

I describe it as swimming in a pool of negativity and we need to have this awareness and then willingness to make adjustments by stepping out of this pool of negativity, shifting our focus off the negative thoughts and onto healthy, positive thoughts based on our most recent evidence that it will be okay.

We know that negative thoughts will lead to negative feelings, negative emotions, and unwanted or dysfunctional behaviors. We know that positive thoughts will lead to positive feelings, positive emotions, and more positive behaviors.

In my private practice, I encourage clients to make a shift in how they view the world. Stepping away from the negative and into the positive. This is more than just positive self talk. Life is not rainbows and unicorns and think positive and everything will be okay. We need evidence in our lives to support the idea that everything will be okay.

We begin by identifying what thoughts are coming in. If it is a negative thought, is it true, if it is true what can you do differently to dispute that negativity. In other words, what can you do differently to make things better? If the thoughts are not true or irrational you do the same thing. Seek out evidence to dispute the negativity. Having some awareness and recognition of our thoughts, allows us to initiate change.

A strategy I often use and have discussed already centers around awareness. Be aware of what is going on, be present but this is not always enough. We can be aware and still be stuck. The next step is the willingness to make adjustments. I do not want anyone to ever feel stuck because there is no reason to be stuck.

Awareness is the first step, but the next step is equally as important. We must be willing to make an adjustment. The willingness to make an adjustment is the action part of this strategy. What will you do differently to make things better? One thing, one thing you can tweak or change to make things better. Look at your daily routine, start there. **What can you do**

differently today within your daily routine to make things better for you? I also suggest extending this to your weekly schedule. **What can you do differently throughout your week to make things better for you?**

As a cognitive-behavioral therapist, I believe strongly in our thought life. Our thought life and observations of others. We learn how to be through our observations of others. We learn how to be, from the environment we were raised in. We call this our learned behaviors. We are the way we are, because we saw, what we saw.

Think about your childhood. How far back can you remember? Take some time to look back within yourself but be careful not to fabricate false memories as you do this. What was the reality of your childhood? Is it difficult to decipher from the real events and what you think you remember about your reality? I know when I try to do this, I get confused. What was real? What have I made up?

We often fabricate memories to "fill in the blanks", to complete a picture that does not quite make sense. We just assume that it must have been that way, how else could it have been? As much as you might think it matters to be accurate and before you start phoning everyone to create a more accurate and complete picture (keep in mind you are phoning people who are faced with the same threat of inserting fabricated memories to complete the picture).

I want to tell you it does not matter. It does not matter if it was fabricated or not. What matters is, this is what you believe, and this is what you have based your life on.

Whether fabricated or not you have attached emotions, values, and beliefs to your observations and memories from the past. So, as I have said, I believe we are shaped by our thoughts and our observations of our environments, and these observations may be true and accurate or maybe partially true and or inaccurate.

Moving on from fabricated memories to thought life. It is helpful to decipher the difference between dysfunctional thoughts and faulty beliefs that are keeping you stuck in the past, and the positive functional thoughts that are true and accurate that will allow you to have an incredible future, and a great life.

Remember, the goal is to stop living life in the 'past lane'. The main point I want you to come away with here is to have an awareness of the thoughts you are having. **What thoughts are keeping you stuck in the past? What thoughts are helping you dispute the negativity from the past?**

At this time, I want to dive deeper into theory and strategies I use. Between the fine line of going crazy and understanding human behavior, I have realized how similar we all are and how explainable behavior is. As a registered psychologist, I now have a life of drawing conclusions. A life of wondering why we are the way we are, what makes us great, or what makes us anxious, depressed, or conflicted.

I often say there is a thread that runs through all of humanity. We can relate to each other because we have similar experiences we live through our emotions. You see someone sad, and you can relate because you have been sad before. You do not necessarily need to know why that person is sad to understand what they are feeling.

If you have traveled to another country where you are not familiar with the language you can still read how people are doing and gain an understanding of how they are doing in that moment. You can read their expressions, and feel the emotions, the energy they are giving off. You can observe an individual or a group and have a fairly accurate read on how they are doing based on your observations. Human behavior and human emotion is universal.

We all feel and experience emotions, and we have discussed how our thoughts influence our emotions. How we cope and manage these thoughts and emotions will impact how our lives go. We want to take initiative, be proactive, be the author of our own stories.

We do not have to live in someone else's script, we do not have to stumble over the past and lose sight of where we hope to land moving forward. We want to gain a better understanding of where we came from so we can do a better job of focusing forward on better days ahead.

Yes, we are shaped by our thoughts and observation of our past experiences but that does not have to define who we are, or who we will become. Choice must play a role. We fall back on what we have learned during times of stress. This is a built-in coping mechanism that we rely on. However, in most instances we are relying on a dysfunctional coping mechanism we learned as children and that is where thinking about thinking comes in.

We do not want to be locked in or trapped in a pattern of using dysfunctional coping strategies when we can gather more relevant, useful, recent evidence and use this evidence to cope and manage in a more productive way. In other words, we can think about it in a different way based on our most recent evidence instead of relying on old coping strategies that are most likely dysfunctional.

Ask yourself next time you are in a difficult situation, "is this response something I learned as a child, as a coping strategy, or is this simply my reaction to the situation based on my current ability to cope and manage my thoughts". In other words, are you reacting in a healthy, functional manner or are you letting past experiences dictate your thoughts, feelings, and behaviors?

Remember that some of our past experiences are based on dysfunctional thoughts and faulty belief systems. Take some time to reflect on this… **Are you operating in the here and now or speeding down the road in the past lane?**

What we may have believed to be true may not be true at all. If someone tells you something enough times, we tend to believe it. The rationale for this is, why would they keep saying it if it was not true? Remember parts of our discussion from before. Sometimes people spew negativity or project their negative dysfunctional way of being on you to cope and manage with their issues and problems.

Our lives need to be about stepping outside of the bubble or box and looking over what we have created for a life. Our wives, husbands, children, friends, family, careers, and activities we enjoy. We need to evaluate and appreciate what we have. Being happy with what we have accomplished, pushing harder with drive and determination for the things we would still like to accomplish, and this is not just about career and material items. It is more about the relationships we form along the way.

Perhaps we want a better relationship with our spouse or our children. Use the same drive and determination you used to be successful in your career to make your relationships successful. I can tell you that all your accomplishments will be meaningless unless you have built some solid relationships along the way.

I have many successful clients that come in miserable, and they cannot explain it. They are at a loss. I ask about the relationships they formed "along the way up" and the response is "well I never really had time for that" and I respond, "well that's why you are so miserable". Relationships need to be a priority in our lives.

Too often we are driven and focused to achieve success, but the target or goal keeps moving so we keep forging ahead until we reach what we consider the top. While we are doing this, we have blinders on. We see nothing and tend to nothing other than the target or goal.

Relationships suffer, marriages end, and children and adolescents' behavior typically takes a turn for the worst but hey, you got that promotion or became wealthier, so it was all worth it right? Wrong. Remember, pay now, or pay later. Too often we forget what is important. We need to step outside of the bubble or box and look over what we have created for a life.

Our wives, husbands, children, friends, family, careers, and activities we enjoy. We need to evaluate and appreciate what we have. Being happy with what we have accomplished, pushing harder with drive and determination for the things we would still like to accomplish and again this is not just about career and material items. Remember, use the same drive and determination you used to be successful to make your relationships successful.

Back to the uncertainty of our thoughts, feelings, behaviors, belief systems, morals, values, etc.... I mentioned earlier, what if they are based on dysfunctional thoughts and faulty belief systems created as coping mechanisms when we were children or adolescents, or what if they are based on our observations of the adults in our lives as we were growing up?

This is where a good therapist comes in. Someone to help you, discover you. Looking deep inside and creating an environment that allows you to dispute and question areas of your life that are conflicted. This is the process of "pulling out the junk and sorting through it". During this process, we discover how we learned to cope with our issues and problems, and this leads me to Freud and his defense mechanisms.

As I noted earlier, during my sessions I discuss many different strategies with my clients. I understand one strategy that may work for one may not work for another. Even though I believe in all the strategies, I understand we need to meet people where they are in hopes of helping them get to a better place. My hope is, through our discussions, that my clients will start to think about things differently than they had before.

Clients are encouraged to process the information we have discussed and utilize the strategies that they most connect with. This is also part of the next session I have with them. Discussing which strategies, they feel are effective for them. Therapy is a partnership, and we work together to find solutions to the problems. My role in this partnership is to guide and support. Tapping into the strategies provided by the work done by Freud has been helpful throughout my career.

Freud was an incredibly wise man. He identified many defense mechanisms that are at the heart of most of our coping strategies. Of course, they are not all appropriate or considered functional because we often rely on them so often, they themselves become dysfunctional. Let us look at a few that I discuss in my sessions.

Let us start with identifying with the aggressor. This is a scenario where you become more like the aggressor as your means of conquering the fear of that person, strange but true. You focus on the negative or feared traits of the person and become more like them; this is an actual defense mechanism.

The thought here is, and this is my opinion only, we are not going to fear something we can be ourselves. Perhaps it is a level of comfort to know that we can step it up and be just as awful as the aggressor therefore we no longer need to fear them. I prefer to call it standing up for yourself and not taking any shit from someone who is probably still being a bully from his/her younger years. One thing to mention quickly about bullies, they have low self-esteem and need to pick on others to feel better about themselves. A good therapist can help with this.

The first defense mechanism that Freud discovered, and arguably the most important was repression. This is the process of keeping disturbing or threatening thoughts from becoming conscious.

Repression, we are pressing them down and away from our awareness. The act of not thinking about it and hoping it goes away. It being a disturbing or threatening thought. You can see the issues and problems this will cause. We cannot ignore or keep thoughts out forever. They find a way in, or they cause us to react in different ways than we normally would. Also remember our discussion about the negative, intrusive thoughts that always seem to be knocking on the door trying to get in and trip us up.

At times, we allow issues to build up until we finally erupt (remember pebbles in the tin bucket). If we deal with our issues, problems, and concerns, we no longer carry them around with us. We can examine them, deal with them, and then move on. Rather than repression, try expression.

Express how you are feeling, talk about your issues, problems, and concerns so you may gain a new perspective. Perspective is paramount in appreciating where you are, what you are dealing with, and the points of view of others.

Take a step back and observe and try and gain a new perspective. Try and identify your defining moment. A time in your life when things were good, to a time in your life when things were not good.

Remember the awareness of what was going on and the willingness to make adjustments to make things better for you. If we attend to the issues, problems, and concerns as they come up we have less to carry around and avoid the consequence of the build up over time scenario we have previously discussed.

Issues, problems, and concerns are contributors to anxiety. Anxiety is one of the biggest issues I deal with in my private practice. I can understand and appreciate this because of the ridiculous pace we set for ourselves. It is nonstop juggling work, family, friends, and activities, and so on, and let us not forget a Global Pandemic.

I also attribute some of the high levels of anxiety to our childhood and adolescent years. We learn to fear, to be anxious about unknowns, the uncertainty of life. I am starting this discussion with my experiences as an adolescent and as with my lengthy introduction to myself, many of the issues, problems, scenarios discussed have a universal commonality. In other words, we can all relate and learn from our experiences and the experiences of others.

Through reflection, I was able to assess my childhood and adolescence. Many of the thoughts and feelings expressed here were foreign to me at the time. I was not emotionally equipped to make these observations of self. However, later in life, I became better equipped to discuss this phase of my life.

Take some time to reflect on your childhood and adolescence and make note of areas of concern. **Are these concerns continuing to impact you today? What did you try to do about these concerns then? What will you try to do about these concerns now?**

Remember we are visiting the past to make sense of it, to gain clarity and get some closure and perhaps most importantly, take the lessons learned and carry them forward. This is not about living life in the past or as I have titled this book, living life in the past lane.

My adolescence was no different than the ones I observed daily as a junior high school teacher. The clothes and hairstyles might have changed along with some of the curriculum, but the anxious feelings I experienced are like the ones I have observed. It was an awkward phase of development that I experienced. Social anxiety often affected how I interacted with others, what extracurricular activities I choose to engage in, and my overall view of the world I lived in.

I can remember times during my adolescence when I would avoid certain activities at school because I was too unsure of myself to participate. Simply stated, I did not want to draw attention to myself or embarrass myself in any way.

Every person has a personal threshold for what they can handle coming at them from the world. If pushed past this threshold by events I was not comfortable with, I would feel stressed, even overwhelmed and as I have explained to many of my clients', anxiety can present as anger, an anger that is often misunderstood.

Having overwhelming social anxiety can be difficult for anyone to manage, particularly youth. I believe social anxiety must be a product of or result of something or someone from the past, present, or future.

In other words, my beliefs about why certain adolescents suffer more from social anxiety than others stems from an event or interaction from the past, present, or anticipating event from the future that has, is, or will overwhelm the individual.

My adolescence was a time of discovery where I was in search of identifying who I was and who I wanted to be. I, like many of my peers, struggled to find this identity. There were times when I was paralyzed with a fear of social situations.

I remember wondering if people were watching me walk, watching me eat, or watching how I would react to the world around me. All this made me very anxious. Thankfully being on a team, whether it was hockey, baseball of football, allowed me to escape into the security of a group/team.

I think the worst times were on the bus, especially when someone would sit across from me. I remember becoming extremely nervous when someone would get on the bus and there was an empty seat beside me. I used to get all worked up in anticipation of this person's selection of seats. I remember the self-talk that occurred during these times. I used to tell myself, "Don't sit here, don't sit here", almost as if my self-talk would influence where this person sat on the bus.

Self-talk is such an important area to discuss and be aware of. Sometimes the self-talk we use, hoping it makes things better, is what is making things worse. **Assess your self-talk so you can determine if it is helpful or hurtful.**

Remember the previous discussion about being a young child riding the bus alone to school. If you remember, this was not the typical yellow bus we often see children riding in, but the city transit. There were regular people on the bus mixed in with students.

I believe this contributed to the anxiety I was feeling at the time. My coping strategy was self-talk and at the time, it may have worked but as we grow and learn more about the world around us we must reassess our coping strategies to determine if they are still appropriate or not.

As an adult, if I am still riding the bus and still scared, nervous and anxious about someone sitting by me or next to me I have an unresolved issue from my past that an old coping strategy acts more like a band aide than a solution to a problem. This is the type of self discovery I hope for my clients. Now, what can I do differently to make things better? Use my most recent evidence that things will be okay.

During my early adolescent years, I experienced the divorce of my parents. This made me feel like even more of an outsider as all my friends' parents were still together. I realize now that this was not a reflection of who I was, or who I would become, but rather the circumstances at that time. Again, two adults could not get along, so they did what they thought was best at the time.

I also experienced a time when I questioned my value or worth with regards to my place in the world. I remember times when I would isolate myself in my room and stare off into the sky and wonder why I had so many racing thoughts in my head all day long. I wondered if "I was crazy" or was "going crazy".

Adolescence was a difficult time for me as I struggled to see where I fit in this world. Luckily for me, I had sports, teachers, and coaches to help me along the way. We need to connect more with our children and adolescents. Communicate more, support them more.

As I mentioned my parents had divorced. My two older brothers remained with my stepfather at the house and my mother, and I moved to low-income housing. I remember feeling abandoned by my brothers. It was confusing. I really could not make sense of how the family was now structured. Again, I remember feeling like an outsider who had now been abandoned by his brothers.

These experiences created or provoked anxious feelings within me. This I believe leads to attachment issues. Trusting that family and friends would "always be there" became a question I often asked myself. I will emphasize here that at the time I did not give it much thought (remember Freud's concept of repression) but as you know we get older and hopefully become more aware. With awareness we can process the concerns from our past and make more sense of what we can do differently to make things better moving forward.

We either repeat the dysfunction of the past or work hard not too. Sometimes this is much easier said than done but a goal we should all have. Live and learn from the past and do a better job moving forward. In this case the goal was not to bury feelings and emotions, but express them, work through them, and land in a better place.

I did not fare much better during my early adulthood years. I was very unsettled. My experiences from my adolescent years dominated my thoughts. My adolescent years seemed to condition me to think, feel and react to my environment in a way that always seemed to be full of anxious thoughts. Thinking back, I still do not know how I could have made things more tolerable. Again, being part of a team helped me fade into the group rather than standout in a crowd.

Hopefully reading this helps you start to think about things differently in your life and creates enough awareness to initiate some change or willingness to make adjustments.

It was during my years as a teacher I began to have a victory over my social anxiety. The battle continues, but I tend to be winning more of the battles. I attribute these successes to my knowledge of Cognitive Therapy. Disputing negative thoughts with evidence it will be okay. The basic premise being that our thoughts influence how we feel and how we behave. By learning to question the validity of my thoughts, whether they were valid or not, and disputing the negative thoughts with evidence it would be okay, were the first steps I incorporated into my daily routine.

As we have discussed, awareness of thought was key and then the willingness to make adjustments was the next important step that needed to be taken. Continuing with my knowledge of Cognitive Therapy I began to ask myself what the worst-case scenario would be if the dysfunctional, negative thoughts I was having were indeed valid. What evidence did I have to support this?

As I often say during our sessions, worst case scenario, as bad as it may initially seem to be, is usually not as bad as we thought. Therapy helps us become better equipped to cope and manage with the ups and downs of life, to navigate more effectively through the challenges we may face. To navigate through the worst-case scenarios, we have created in our thought lives.

Remember the example about the student who was concerned about failing an exam. What is the worst-case scenario? Failing the exam. So, what if you fail the exam? You rewrite it. Worst case scenario is not that bad. It is not best-case scenario, but it certainly is not worst-case scenario.

We want to be actively involved in our thought life. It is not a runaway train that gets to dictate every move we make. We are in more control and have more power than we realize. Thinking about thinking and doing something about the negative, intrusive, dysfunctional thoughts is within our control. We have the power to make things better.

Usually, after the first session, I have clients do a homework assignment. It is to gain an awareness of the thoughts coming in, the recognition of the thoughts they are having. The awareness and recognition of thought is an important piece used in cognitive therapy. I want clients to think about thinking.

We have more than 6000 thoughts a day, and of course, these numbers are always up for debate. I am not asking clients to become aware of every thought they have. I am asking clients to become aware of the thoughts that are causing them to feel bad, sad, scared, nervous, depressed, and anxious.

If it is causing you negative emotion, identify it, catch it, check it, and change it. Identify the harmful thoughts and do something about them. Again, awareness and willingness to make adjustments.

Reading the available research has made me aware of some aspects that I had not thought about before. Recall bias, the act of recalling the negative aspects of a situation or event was a concept I was unaware of. I had experienced this phenomenon personally but had never had a formal understanding of what it was. This is not a phenomenon that was easily understood.

After an interaction with a peer or authority figure, I would ruminate over what was said and evaluate how I handled myself within that situation. As time would pass, I would continue to dwell on the interaction and would often only focus on the negative aspects of the interaction.

In other words, I would question what I said and why I said it and wondered or questioned myself about how the interaction went because in my mind it did not go well. There had been times when I would recreate the verbal portions of an interaction verbatim to determine how it went. I believe this was a coping strategy to help me decrease my level of anxiety.

As I have engaged in many discussions with my clients regarding anxiety and what their experience has been regarding anxiety, many report a similar reaction at one time or another. Think about a time when you have done this and look at the evidence you can take away from this experience. We want to learn that this recall bias or focusing on what we have perceived as being a negative exchange, had more to do with our anxiety than the actual exchange. In other words, we are trying not to overthink and over analyze the interactions we have with others.

The physiological reactions I experienced as an adolescent included a racing heart before and during events or interactions, shaking hands during class presentations, muscle tension, blushing, and confusion.

Of course, at the time I never attributed these characteristics to social anxiety but now I have a better understanding, through researching this area, that these characteristics were symptoms of social anxiety.

The stomach problems I have experienced over the years can also be linked to my anxiety. According to the DSM-IV-TR (2000) "individuals with Social Phobia almost always experience symptoms of anxiety (e.g., palpitations, tremors, sweating, gastrointestinal discomfort, diarrhea, muscle tension, blushing and confusion) in the feared social situation" (*DSM-IV-TR*, 2000, p. 451).

The anticipatory anxiety (situations/contexts) that I can recall included walking to the bus stop, getting on the bus, finding a spot to sit on the bus, riding on the bus worrying if someone was going to sit beside me, and getting off the bus once I had reached my destination. Most, if not all of this can be attributed to my anticipation of unknown factors. The questions regarding the situations would be racing through my mind as I would fear that others were watching me or evaluating every move I made. Remember we are trying hard not to overthink and over analyze. The more we overthink and over analyze a situation, the worse it becomes.

Here is an example to consider. Friday your child comes home, and all is good. You have a good weekend; they have a good weekend. Sunday night your child does not feel well. We often hear about school refusal being a defiant behavior. Some comment that "my child hates school" or "I go through this every weekend, trying to get my child ready to go to school on Monday". So, what do you think the problem is here?

When we dwell on negative thoughts it stirs up negative emotions, feelings and influences our behaviors. As we have learned it even creates physiological reactions like school refusal. Your child may seem defiant because they have social anxiety. They may be overthinking, over analyzing, and becoming overwhelmed about school.

Fridays are fine, Mondays are awful. I have worked with many adolescent clients who experienced this. Here we lean on one of our strategies we have discussed. Use evidence in your life to dispute the negative thoughts. Pump the brakes on the negative thoughts and focus on your evidence that you have that it will be okay. Awareness and the willingness to make adjustments. Once we recognize a pattern we can correct the dysfunctional parts of this pattern.

School is the one place or one thing our children and adolescents know better than anything else. They have been "doing school" their whole lives. It should be the most comfortable place they go each day but as we know this is not always the case. When you are experiencing social anxiety, you are on high alert, overthinking every move you make and sometimes overthinking every move others are making as well. So, we try and cope the best way we can.

We cope the best way we can, I would try and hide or fade into the business of the school setting. I did not want to be noticed in the hallways, classrooms, or anywhere else for that matter. I just wanted to be invisible because I was so fearful that others were judging or evaluating me. When I would walk the hallways as a teacher, counsellor, or administrator I would watch for this and try to provide support to students who were visibly uncomfortable with the school environment. This is an example of awareness and a willingness to make an adjustment to make things better for someone else.

Gaining an understanding of what others may be going through is an important step in providing appropriate supports for that person. This happens either through effectively communication with that person (remember communication, understanding, support) or by reflecting on your own experiences and using this information to help you understand what others may be going through.

Moving from the hallways and into the classroom, presenting a report in class seemed like a life-ending endeavor. Even answering a question asked by the teacher made me uncomfortable. "Exposure to the social or performance situation almost invariably provokes an immediate anxiety response" (*DSM-IV-TR*, 2000, p. 450). Sometimes when a student does not want to answer it may be due to social anxiety and not that they do not know the answer. Give students different ways to show you what they know.

We have often discussed in staff meeting and during many professional development opportunities the importance of differentiation. The importance of teaching our students in different ways because we know they do not all learn the same way. Assessing students also needs to follow this concept. Some students do very well writing an essay, some are good at multiple choice, others are great at oral presentations. Offer students a variety of different ways to demonstrate what they have learned.

Most of my experiences as an adolescent with social anxiety provide examples of anxiety-ridden thinking. Even these examples are evidence that my thinking was riddled with anxiety. The dysfunctional thoughts that dominated my thinking patterns directly increased my levels of anxiety.

Anxiety-ridden thinking supported the fears that I was experiencing. The thoughts seemed to validate my fear. A specific example of anxiety-ridden thinking that dominated most of my life is when I would sit down to eat in front of others. I used to think that everyone was watching me. I used to think that perhaps I did not deserve to be eating, or I was chewing my food too many times. I realize now that this fear was excessive and/or unreasonable, but at the time it was very real to me.

This is yet another example of overthinking and over analyzing. I believe we all do this from time to time and we need to shift this focus off overthinking and over analyzing using the strategy of pumping the brakes and using evidence from our inventory to help us understand that it will be okay.

Shift away from the overthinking and over analyzing and on to the 'that was then, and this is now' and 'everything is going to be okay' self talk that can be helpful in these situations. Again, not a "rainbows and unicorns" fairy tale but using evidence you have in your life to dispute the negative, intrusive thoughts that are holding you back from having a better life.

During my adolescence, I did not fully understand what anxiety was. I had no definition or concept of what anxiety was. Back then we always heard about children and adolescents that worried too much. Well, that is just another way of saying they had anxiety. I now have a better understanding of what anxiety is and the symptoms associated with it.

I know that Social Phobia is referred to as Social Anxiety and by using the *DSM-IV-TR* (2000) I have furthered my understanding of what it involves. I know that social anxiety can impair daily activities. This I have observed and experienced at various times in my life. I know social anxiety can affect how we view the world around us. In other words, an increase in the cognitive distortions we experience.

Reading the available research on the topic of anxiety has confirmed my belief that it is a result of something or someone from the past or the anticipation of something that is unknown or uncertain. I know that some cases of social anxiety are lifelong but believe seeking out treatment can be a way of coping with the disorder. The identification of coping strategies is an important element to consider. Personally, this has been effective for me and my clients.

Let us dive deeper into social anxiety and what it is and what we can do about it. Remember we discussed asking ourselves what we could do differently to make things better? I will discuss some strategies that may help you or your loved one's cope better.

The essential features, specific culture, age and gender features, prevalence, course, and familial patterns of Social Anxiety disorders are defined below using the *DSM-IV-TR,* (2000).

> *Social Phobia is a marked and persistent fear of social or performance situations in which embarrassment may occur. Clinical presentation and resulting impairment may differ*

across cultures, depending on social demands. Young children exhibit behaviors such as crying, tantrums, freezing, clinging, or staying close to a familiar person. Social Phobia typically has an onset in the mid-teens, sometimes emerging out of a childhood history of social inhibition or shyness. Onset may abruptly follow a stressful or humiliating experience, or it may be insidious. The course of Social Phobia is often continuous. Duration is frequently life-long, although the disorder may attenuate in severity or remit during adulthood. Social Phobia appears to occur more frequently among first-degree biological relatives of those with the disorder compared with the general population (DSM-IV-TR, 2000, p. 450-453).

The definition of Social Anxiety is a great place to start in understanding what Social Anxiety entails. Sorry to throw a hardcore definition at you but it is important to understand that anxiety or social anxiety is real, and it really can limit our lives to the point that we withdraw and isolate ourselves and as we withdraw and isolate ourselves we may become lonely and depressed.

I work with clients to open-up their worlds again. To give them access to the world they have withdrawn from. Earlier I discussed previous experiences, how we were or are shaped by our observations from the past. Welcome to the formation of anxiety, our past experiences.

Anxiety, in my opinion, is a learned behavior, therefore it can be unlearned. We learn to be anxious at a young age or at a different phase of life and this carries forward and creates a barrier or wall that shields us from perceived dangers that may or may not be real. Cognitive therapy helps examine this, looking for evidence to dispute the dysfunctional thoughts and faulty beliefs attached to the thoughts.

The most common example I use with adolescents who struggle with anxiety is my conversations regarding test anxiety as demonstrated in this next scenario. Another example of how we need to use our evidence that things will be okay.

Students come to me worried they are going to fail their exam. I ask them if they studied, reviewed notes, attended class, asked questions in class, and generally paid attention. Usually, they respond with yes, yes, I did all those things or most of those things. I respond by telling them they just provided evidence to contradict their thought about failing the exam.

Thoughts are powerful and too often we accept them as truth rather than question and dispute them. What evidence do you have that the thought is true, what evidence do you have that the thought is not true. We need to actively do this because dysfunctional thoughts that automatically pop into our heads throughout the day are not always accurate, and these dysfunctional thoughts will cause us to feel differently and act differently. Dispute negative thoughts with evidence it will be okay.

I have discussed the "defining moment" that we all need to identify at some point in our lives to gain an understanding of why things changed, why we are the way we are. Really, the contributing factors that brought us to this place today. Through some careful and deliberate reflection, I discovered one of the defining moments that helped me understand when and why I became anxious as a child/adolescent.

It seems so obvious now, but this is a discovery for me. The separation and divorce of my mother and stepfather. That was it. The big aha moment. My world changed and now there was reason to doubt and have uncertainty and unknowns dominate my thinking. **What have you discovered about your defining moment or defining moments in your life?**

I want to continue this discussion by talking about adult issues from childhood experiences. Ozzy Osbourne is a brilliant man. "Riding down the rails on the crazy train". How simple a statement, how true it is? We have adolescents all going through the same issues that are desperately trying to be different and then we have adults who are different who are trying to be the same. Indeed, riding down the rails on the crazy train.

Humans are remarkably interesting. How we think, how we act, how we perceive, what we choose to focus on, what becomes vital to our existence, all very fascinating. We get locked into something and convince ourselves we cannot live without it.

Advertisers take advantage of us every day. The way to combat this is to remove the emotional drive behind the desire and take a rational, logical approach. This may sound boring and uninspiring, but it will save you thousands of dollars. The Global Pandemic is an example I can use here. If you watch the news for an hour you are informed by it, if you watch the news 24/7 you are consumed by it.

Remember thought life is powerful. The bible talks about guarding your thought life. Guard your thought life against the negativity. Dispute negativity with evidence it will be okay. Again, watch the news to be informed, do not be consumed by the news because you have watched too much of it.

When we dwell on negativity it changes us and takes us somewhere we do not want to go. Remember if you are thinking about cold beer all day the odds that you are having a cold beer when you get home are high. Same concept, the more we think about something the more likely we are to do it. This can be positive and help us succeed, or it can be negative and trip us up.

I stated that adolescents are going through the same issues but at the same time trying to be different and this is an important point, but I do want to clarify that I am not saying adolescents all go through the same issues at the same time. Adolescents hit certain phases at different times but within these phases, they experience similar issues.

Issues like searching for an identity, finding good friends, fitting in somewhere. There are also issues related to growth such as height, weight, hygiene, and developing mentally and physically. If we focus too much on what we perceive as issues within ourselves or focus on areas that we feel inferior when compared to others, then we are missing the big picture of life. Dwelling on the negative will take us to a negative place. A place we do not want to go.

"Dysfunctional thoughts keep this dysfunction alive."

What makes us think we are so special that we are the only ones going through this? If as an adolescent we are having these thoughts, it is not a big stretch to recognize that other adolescents are also having these thoughts or similar thoughts.

Dysfunctional thoughts keep this dysfunction alive. We think "no one understands me, no one could understand what I am going through". This is dysfunctional. If we are all humans, and we have all developed through childhood, adolescence into adulthood why is it that there is a perception from adolescents that no one will understand?

It is the egocentrism of adolescents that allows this lack of understanding of others to flourish. We are all different, yet we are all the same. We are all the same, yet we are all different. No wonder children, adolescents, and even adults are so confused about life. It is confusing.

Adolescents need us to understand them at face value. Meet them, and others, where they are. Understand them in the absolute here and now because it is the here and now that adolescents are most focused on. Adults can understand because we have been down that road, experienced a similar journey. We have or should have wisdom. We should live and learn from our past and try to do a better job moving forward.

If we learn nothing from our past, then we have been wasting our time and not paying attention. Live and learn from our past and try to do a better job moving forward. Hopefully, this is a theme you picked up on throughout this book. Moving forward, not dwelling on or being stuck in the past. Focus forward on better days ahead. Do not live life in the past lane.

Think about it this way. If you are driving your car and you only focus on where you have been, in other words, focused on what is in the rear-view mirror, you will crash, have an accident, not see where you are going. Focus forward on where you want to go, not on where you have been. We were there already; we took the parts and pieces that will help us grow and change and left the rest behind.

The goal is to live and learn from the past and do a better job moving forward based on those lessons we have learned. Again, if we have learned nothing from our past mistakes and or experiences, we have been wasting our time and have not been paying attention.

Shifting gears from my work with clients struggling with anxiety I would like to discuss the work I do with couples. Couple's counselling is great for exploring what works and what does not work within a relationship. Many of the strategies discussed can be used with any relationship you are involved in such as, friends, family and even coworkers.

Couple's counseling is an area that I have grown to love over the years. There is nothing better than helping a couple reconnect and find happiness once again. Growing to love an area like this has not come without its challenges. Change is difficult and again we base so much of our behaviors on what we have learned from our environments growing up. What we saw, what we heard, the behaviors of others not only in our homes but on tv and in movies.

What I found is the issues are all the same and I will go into this in detail because it is important to realize that you are not alone. I know by saying "the issues are all the same" will cause an uproar but let us be honest, they are.

Couples fight about money, communication, infidelity, lost hopes and dreams, sex, family, friendships, driving, walking, sitting, you name it, I have heard it all. Your marriage is not the only bad one. Your husband or wife is not the biggest mistake you ever made.

We cannot allow the isolation of our marriage to drop seeds of doubt into our thoughts and feelings we have about our partners. It is not fair; it is not accurate, and it is not helpful. I want to go through some of the items on the list above and have you consider the parallels in your marriage.

Finances are a big deal. We fight about money. We agonize about money. We cheat, lie, steal, and manipulate for money. We want money and we stress about needing it, wanting it, and getting it.

Money is one of those external factors that comes in and ruins your relationship. It has no business in there, but it comes in anyway and drives a wedge between the two of you. Imagine you and your partner are in a bubble and within that bubble you have some issues, but you talk about them before there is a build-up over time, so generally speaking it is pretty darn good if no other stressors come along.

Now in comes money. Bubbles a bit more crowded, and not as manageable as it was before. Here comes the issue. You and your partner are different yet very much the same. You are different because you have different backgrounds, different environments that you were exposed to growing up, different influences in your life, different characteristics, personalities, thoughts, and opinions, and so on.

You are the same because you both want to have some level of success, financial security. You want to have a happy family, good friends, and vacation opportunities and the list can go on and on. So here is the major problem.

We can all admit that we are different as explained above and we can all admit that we are the same in the sense that we have similar interests in being happy, finding success, etc. Where everything goes sideways is the lack of communication about all these factors.

We are not on the same page, same chapter, same book, same team, and some would argue not even from the same planet. Remember communication, understanding, and support, the model discussed earlier.

Couples need to talk about what they need and what that looks like. The tricky part of this is our needs change over time, so often we make assumptions that what he or she needed before is what they need now. So, we do not understand or do not take the time to understand what it is that they need now. Instead, we get upset, mad, angry, and shut down. Does this sound familiar to you?

So, what do we do? We argue we fight, and we continue to be in a state of conflict. As a society, we take two people and put them under the same roof or in this case the same bubble and we say okay, get along... Does not work! Never has, never will. This is a recipe for disaster unless we bridge the gap somehow. Unless we figure out how we are and how our partner is and gain a true understanding of who we are together.

The only way to do this is by communicating. Who are we together? What are our strengths, weaknesses, triggers, hotspots, areas of concern, areas that bring us joy and happiness? This is all important stuff and if we never talk about it, it will become another area of conflict. Soon there is nothing left. There is nothing left to talk about that does not trigger a conflict.

Now you come in to see a professional. This is a tough decision to make, but you want help and what do you say when you finally come in, "You are our last hope, and if you can't fix this we are done". I have honestly heard this statement several times.

My response to this is if two people are committed and willing to put in some time and effort that there are areas that we can make better, but you must be willing to do more than just come in once a week for a session. Remember something we have discussed before. If you are willing to put in the time and effort there is nothing that you cannot accomplish.

The important work begins once you leave my office. What we need to create is an environment that encourages effective communication that does not attack, criticize, or judge the other. Communicate about what you need and what that would look like because most of the disagreements are about misunderstandings due to a lack of communication.

As I said before if the couple is willing to put in the time and effort, we have a shot at making the relationship better. The key phrase I often use is to look for the evidence. Look for evidence that he/she, each day, is putting in an effort to make the relationship better in some way. Evidence of an effort, evidence of change. If you see it, you have a chance. If you do not see it, why don't you see it?

Some men say, "I forgot, it was such a busy week". Nice try. We are all busy. Think about your priorities. Make a list and prioritize the list. If you are religious your list might look like this: God, Husband/Wife, Children, Extended Family, Friends, Hobbies/Activities, Work. Notice something interesting about this list. Where is work? Work is last on this list. Why? Because everything ahead of it is more important for your mental and physical health, your overall well-being, your hope for happiness.

When your priorities are in the right order life is good. When your priorities are out of order your life is not good. That is the simplest way I can put it. Get your priorities in the right order and live your life in a way that provides evidence that you know where your priorities are. When you have a decision to make, think about how that decision will impact your priorities.

I counsel my couples to pick something they can do consistently. Something they can sustain over a long period of time (really until the end of time). There is nothing worse than giving your spouse some hope of a better relationship by providing evidence of change and then stopping.

Stopping because life got busy with work, children, friends, family, the external factors that drive a wedge between the two of you. Remember the bubble. It needs to be the two of you. The external factors must be independent of the relationship. Do not get mad at your spouse because the taxes are due, and you have no money. Have a conversation (not a conflict) about how we, as a team, as partners, can figure this out. No blaming, no conflicts, just a plan.

What is the one thing you can do differently today, this week, this month, to make things better for you? What is the one thing we can do differently to better support each other? What is it that you need and what does that look like? Ask questions to yourself and your partner. Be curious about what you can do differently to make things better.

If you just sit around hoping things get better, then you are just sitting around hoping. As we have discussed before, you need to be proactive, take some initiative. This is your story to write, no one else's. Make your life and your relationship what you want it to be, what you need it to be.

Focus on the content of the message not on how the message is making you feel. We cannot control what other people say but we can control our reaction to what is said. Remember, not everything said, is a personal attack on you.

It comes down to how we choose to react. Admittedly, this is difficult because emotion is involved, but in time the way we react becomes a part of who we are. Emotionally driven conversations are dangerous. We say things, we do things, and while under the influence of emotion, that tends to make things worse. Simply stated, emotionally driven conversations tend to bury us under a pile of hurt feelings, resentment, and anger.

People who profess to be calm in their demeanor and then have outbursts of anger are fooling themselves. They are not calm; they are just not dealing with anything (most of the time). Remember the build up over time (pebbles in the bucket). We need to pay attention, be aware, and make appropriate adjustments.

Too often you may be blaming others for how you feel or how you are reacting. You believe it is their fault, but if you take a closer look at how you are reacting, and at what exactly you are reacting to, you may realize that your reaction is unwarranted.

The message I want you to take from this last section is to please try and provide evidence, each day, that you are putting in an effort to make the relationship better and be able to sustain these efforts for as long as it takes to push through the difficult times you are experiencing.

Remember not all roads are paved, sometimes we have to travel through the bumpy gravel roads to get to the pavement. If you are willing to put in the time and effort there is nothing you cannot accomplish.

Back to finances. We all have issues and problems with money. I have heard it all. Even the ones that have lots of money and lots of success. The concerns are never ending. I will explain this.

We all have expectations about what we hope for. We need to share these expectations with our spouses. Get on the same page with finances. Have a common account. I call it "the pot". All the money goes into the pot. From the pot the bills get paid, you distribute the money where the money needs to go. You must have a budget. You must work on this together. It is about compromise.

I wrote earlier about couples being from different backgrounds, different environments that you were exposed to, different influences on your life, different characteristics, personalities, thoughts, and opinions, and so on. How do you coexist with so many differences?

The answer is to compromise. A willingness to compromise is probably more accurate. We must be willing to compromise our position, our thoughts, and our feelings about certain subject matter. Consider it more an appreciation for what your partner has to say rather than an issue or a problem because you do not agree.

It is not about biting your tongue and picking your battles (although there are certainly times when this needs to be done). However, picking your battles has an extremely negative tone to it. We want to have a more positive approach to this. We want to compromise because we love our spouse, and really in the big picture, this issue most likely does not matter as much as it does within that moment in time. This is often the case with money.

Really in the big picture does this "issue" matter that much that you are willing to fight all night or all week about it. Is it worth having resentment and anger with you for days, weeks, months, or even years? If we are being honest we would all say no, but we are selfish and stubborn and just want our way whether it makes sense or not.

We need more conversation and less conflict. We should not fight about money because the money comes and goes. Sometimes we have enough sometimes we do not. That is, it. Now how you manage yourself during these times is key. Do not panic, you are in this with your best friend, your spouse, the one person you can count on no matter how bad life gets. Have a budget, stick to it.

I see the budget in the same way I see losing weight. Burning off more than you take in helps you lose weight, spending more than you make will put you into debt. It is not how much you make it is how much you spend. It is all about not overextending yourselves. Credit can be great, but it can also be a relationship killer. Just another external factor that can and will drive a wedge between you and your spouse.

I am not a financial expert so I will just leave you with this. If you save more and spend less you will be fine, but please do not let finances be that external factor that drives a wedge between you and your spouse.

Moving on now from finances and money, I will say that communication is the number one issue that comes up in couples counseling. Despite talking about it second, it is the number one problem we all need to improve on.

If you do not have effective communication, you will not succeed in having a happy relationship. You may be in a relationship right now that has this problem, so you know what I am talking about.

Always arguing, fighting, conflict, no room for error, walking on eggshells, no intimacy, no fun. No hope for a happy life when you look forward to next week, next month, or next year. All you see is misery. Welcome to a relationship that does not have effective communication and here is the kicker, you may be financially stable, but you are not happy. So not even money can save you here.

Just picture this for a minute. You are in a relationship with no effective communication, and you have no money. Double whammy, ouch. Two giant external factors are now causing trouble in your relationship, driving a wedge between the two of you. Now you drift apart, stop caring and eventually break up. I do not want this to happen so let us do something different to make this work. Do not take what your spouse says as a personal attack on you. I understand this is a difficult task, but it is necessary to move forward and get to a better place in your relationship.

Remember parts of our discussion regarding emotionally driven conversations and the dangers of what is being said and done during those exchanges. We say things and do things we regret. Keeping this in mind, it is not a big leap to see that during an argument we say and do things we regret due to the emotionally driven environment we find ourselves in. **Is your spouse attacking you or expressing, whether in a dysfunctional way or not, how hurt they are?**

So, is it a personal attack on you or your partner expressing how hurt they are and how they desperately want things to be better? We do not always know what to do or what to say and again remember some of our previous discussions. We often fall back on what we know/have learned from our past. When we are consumed with stress in an emotionally driven exchange, we often fall back on what we know, and what we would hear growing up.

Remember we want to live and learn and do a better job moving forward. Self-talk comes into play here. Is this about you or them? Can you soften your heart enough to listen and try to gain an understanding of where they are and what they need? Communication, understanding, and support. The more you can gain an understanding of where they are and what they need and what that would look like, the better you can support them where they are.

I made a point earlier that we are shaped by our pasts, the observation we make as children defines who we are and who we will become. We have choices we can make. I knew nothing about relationships or effective communication, and this could be my excuse for unsuccessful relationships, or I could accept the issues and problems from my past and make a choice to have a better life.

I will be the first to admit that I tend to always take the hard road. I was a horrible student but succeeded. I was horrible at communicating my thoughts, feeling and emotions but found a way to succeed at that as well. Time and effort continues to be the strategy that has worked for me. It was not easy, but it was well worth it.

Men are not historically great communicators especially when they have no one to mentor them. I had teachers and coaches but that was school and sports. No one prepares you for relationships more than the parents in your own house. Children and adolescents are watching you. How you talk, act, react, and deal with issues. The way you deal with disappointments, manage anger, and manage conflict. You are not in a bubble alone anymore once you have children. Children can see you and children can feel the stress and tension within the house.

Learning how to communicate would be key. In my case, I had to learn how to communicate more effectively and not take everything as a personal attack. I attribute this to all the years of being alone and not having anyone around to communicate with. I also did not have anyone around telling me what to do so once we enter a relationship and we are no longer alone we must think and act differently than ever before. This was a big change from what I was used to.

Women, for the most part, are better at communicating than men, and this skill set is something we can learn from. Women, as effective communicators, naturally embrace the role of leader when given the opportunity to demonstrate what they know, and what they can do.

The problem I have seen, is this is often interpreted in a way that portrays women as angry, mean, and hostile. I know that sounds harsh, but it has some truth to it. Many of the men I have worked with in my private practice have commented that their wives are controlling, and they do not like that.

Remember, we are still focusing on the importance of communication and what we can do differently to make things better. Ask your self this, is your wife or spouse being controlling or just trying to manage life the best way they know how. Instead of being critical and judgmental perhaps we can all be more understanding and supportive.

If we continue to operate under the umbrella that everything happens for a reason and we want to be curious about what we can do differently to make things better, let this guide us through the next part of our discussion.

If a woman is controlling, there is a reason for that. My theory is it is a defense mechanism that some women use to avoid getting hurt or abused. If they are in control, they know they can manage. Take some of the control away and they feel insecure and threatened. I think we can all relate to this. Especially if there has been exposure to abusive people or abusive environments in our lives.

We all act the way we do for a reason, and unless we make conscious choices to act differently, we allow our past to influence our present and our future. Remember to dispute negativity with evidence in our lives that it will be okay.

I want to make another important note about my belief about women being better equipped to manage challenges in life than men. Again, this may be a controversial thing to say but let us face it women are smart, capable, competent, and fierce competitors. They are also better communicators, and we can learn a lot from them.

Within a relationship we can learn a lot from each other if we are willing to listen and learn and embrace our strengths and help shore up our weaknesses. A marriage is not a competition. We need to stop keeping score. "I did this, well I did that." Conversations like this lead no where.

Remember a marriage is a partnership. You are on the same team. If the team is going to be successful you must work together to achieve your goals. Have a shared vision moving forward and work hard to get there.

If you look at the countries around the world that currently have women leading their countries and you see how they have handled the Global Pandemic, this is recent evidence that supports what I am saying.

If guys are being honest, we know this is true. We have our moments, we achieve, we have successes, but we are reckless, distracted and misguided most of the time. Again, I feel like it has a lot to do with how we were raised.

We were never raised to have emotion or show emotion, in fact, we were often punished for showing any emotion. Does this sound familiar, "stop crying or I'll give you something to cry about." We must all live and learn from our past and try and do a better job moving forward.

Think about this. We cannot go back in time and learn how to communicate better or learn how to better express ourselves but what we can do is make different choices about how we react and respond to the world around us.

Anything that had a negative impact on you as a child should be the things you avoid doing or saying now that you are an adult. Simple, but effective.

As noted early, during my childhood I did not have parents that communicated effectively, worked through problems to find solutions, or work together as a team. As parents we must model the behavior we want to see in our children. This helps them grow and develop into adults that can cope and manage more effectively.

As we have been discussing, communication is the most important skill we can teach our children. This of course will take time and effort but as we have said, you can pay now or pay later. We all have choices we need to make.

Working with couples can be a complex endeavor. They all come in with their own stories, backgrounds, whether good or bad, areas that need to be explored. I encourage couples to work together. I will provide an example of how I start with my couples, even with some of the most difficult cases I have had.

The one thing I believe couples coming into therapy can agree upon is they both would like the relationship to be better that it is right now. They may not know what that looks like yet, but they can surely agree that this can be a good starting point.

So, there you have it, right out of the gate we have a couple who are struggling, who are now agreeing about a starting point. This is our first small victory in our journey to a better relationship.

So, here we are at the starting line and yes this is just the beginning, but it already feels a bit better to agree on something. This may seem like something so small but when you are in a relationship full of conflict and disagreements, it is actually nice to agree on something, even as simple as wanting the relationship to be better.

The couple agree that they would both like the relationship to be better than it is right now. I think this can be a goal for all of us. Always, each day, look at what you can do differently to make things better in your relationship.

Now that we are at the starting line we talk about what we need and what that would look like. Many stop at "what do you need", but what I have discovered is telling someone what you need is not enough. We need to know what that would look like. So, we say, what do you need and what would that look like.

Here is an example of how this usually goes.

Rather than ask for a list of items that you need and then another list of what that would look like, we start with one thing. What is the one thing you need to make the relationship better for you?

One item is more manageable than a long list. If the list is long we often feel overwhelmed and end up doing nothing.

I will use some made up names here, so it is easier to follow. We will use Bill and Mary.

"Mary, what is the one thing you need from Bill to make the relationship better for you?" The typical response from women is communication. "The one thing I need from Bill to make the relationship better for me is more communication."

Now looking over at Bill, he responds with "okay, absolutely, I can do that". Bill at this point has no idea what communicating more would look like for Mary. He is just willing to talk more. Can you see how this does not necessarily solve any of the problems. Can you see how Mary is asking for something, Bill is agreeing to do it, but it has not been defined. If we left it here it would be the next item they fought about.

Mary: "We went to therapy, and I told you what I needed, and you are not doing it".

Bill: "I am doing it; I am talking more than I ever have before".

This may be true but with out defining what communicating more looks like for Mary we are missing the target. We must discuss what we need and what that would look like.

"Mary, what would more communication look like for you?"

Mary: "What I mean by more communication is, when Bill gets home he says hello, how was your day? He shows some kind of interest in how I am doing."

So, as you can see, communicating more for Mary is more than Bill just talking more. We must include what communicating more looks like.

For Mary, there was something missing. Everyday when Bill would come home and not engage with her, there was a build up over time. A build up of resentment and anger. A growing feeling of loneliness. Feeling alone in a marriage. Too often couples drift apart for a variety of reasons. The busyness of life, work, children, family, friends, activities, drugs, and alcohol abuse. The list goes on and on. We need to pay attention because sometimes this is a slow drift, and we find ourselves somewhere we never thought we would be.

My point here is something as basic as communication, something we should all recognize as being important in a relationship, is often the biggest issue we are facing within our marriages.

Now it is Bill's turn.

"Bill, what is the one thing you need from Mary to make the relationship better for you?"

Bill: "I do not know. I never thought about it before. Mary is great. I could not ask for more."

I get this response from men more than any other response. It is our way of avoiding. Avoiding a conflict instead of engaging in a solution to the problem. Even though we are in a safe place to discuss issues and problems and seek out solutions to the problems, Bill is not ready to open up. We need to trust more in the relationship. The environment you create with your partner should be the safest environment in your world.

I had a younger lady in her twenties ask me if it was too much to ask for her partner to be loving, caring, supportive, attentive, respectful, and engaging. I said of course this is not too much to ask, it is the bare minimum, do not ever settle for anything less. Do not feel like this is an unrealistic expectation and you are asking for something that is unattainable. Seeking anything less, than what has been listed here, would most likely indicate that you have lowered your standards, your expectations of what a relationship should be for you, in order to be with someone who you probably should not be with.

Be aware of what you need and what that would look like. Pay attention to the red flags. Anyone who tries to intimidate you, gain power over you, talk down to you, make you feel inadequate; this person cannot be in your life. Do not settle. Know what you want and what that would look like. If you do not know what you are looking for you will find all the wrong people.

I believe when you are with the right person the best parts of you come out. When you are with the wrong person the worst parts of you come out. Think about this more. In your current relationship, are the best parts of you allowed to come out and flourish or are the worst parts of you coming out because you are being consumed with the negativity of your partner. Again, when you are with the right person the best parts of you come out. When you are with the wrong person the worst parts of you come out.

No one gets to have power over you. No one gets to talk down to you. No one gets to make you feel like less of a person. This is not okay, and it leads to abusive, dysfunctional relationships. Sometimes you need to walk away and do what is best for you.

Back to Bill and Mary and the beginning of couples counseling. As I discussed earlier, Bill's response was typical of someone who was not ready to open up and discuss what he needed in the relationship from Mary. Often we view this as being selfish, so we hesitate to ask for anything. We sometimes think "it is not about what I need or want but about what they need or want." I say it is both. It is equally important that both have their needs met. That both get to have a voice and get to express what they need and what that would look like. Think about that one thing you need that would make things better for you?

Communication helps us hit the target. We become more accurate by effectively communicating and effectively listening. Once we gain an understanding of what our partner needs, and we gain an understanding of what it would look like, we can be more supportive. Remember, communication, understanding, support.

Here is another scenario to think about.

Husband gets up early and mows the lawn, cleans up the yard and the garage and is proud of his accomplishments. Wife barely notices and may or may not even acknowledge these efforts. Husband gets upset, "you never appreciate anything I do around here". Wife is blindsided, not understanding where this is coming from.

Often we put in time and effort but in the wrong place. We may think we are doing something for the other person or think this will make the other person happy, but if we are aiming for the wrong target it will not matter what we are doing, it will not be effective.

My point here is this. We discussed putting in time and effort and with time and effort we can accomplish anything however, if the time and effort is put into the wrong areas we gain nothing.

If this scenario does not get discussed it becomes the beginning of resentment and anger that will brew and destroy the relationship because one things leads to another and it will not just be the lawn and yard and garage clean up that is perceived as not being appreciated, it becomes everything as the husband stated, "you never appreciate anything I do around here".

This is all or nothing thinking or a dysfunctional way of thinking about a situation. This is what happens when we engage in an emotionally driven conversation. Instead of this we need to dial things down, go for a walk, cool down, calm down and rethink this whole scenario.

A couple words we should not use are never and always. You will find that no matter when or where you use these words, within your relationship, you will be wrong.

"You never appreciate anything I do around here". This statement is wrong.

"You always come home in a bad mood". This statement is wrong.

Why are these statements wrong? We never, never do something, and tell me a time that something always happens (remember this is within your relationship). If you are being honest with yourself you will see my point here. Please avoid using the words never and always in you emotionally driven "conversations" with you spouse. This may spare you a conflict.

Rethinking this scenario. We will welcome back Bill and Mary for this.

Bill is outside mowing the lawn, cleaning up the yard and garage. In his mind, the way he is thinking about this is "I'm doing such a great job, she is going to love this when she see's it". He is setting himself up for failure.

Bill comes into the house, and we have all seen the puffed-out chest man walk before, and says to Mary "hey, look at the lawn, the yard and the garage, it is awesome". Mary barely acknowledges these efforts. Bill gets upset. Here is where we do a better job, by communicating more effectively. Instead of getting mad let us do as the script that follows.

Bill: "Mary, you do not seem happy with the work I have done. I put in a lot of time and effort to make you happy. You do not seem to appreciate my efforts."

Mary: "Bill, I do appreciate the hard work you do around here but these efforts, if they were for me, missed the target. I would have preferred spending time with you rather than you doing the lawn, the yard and the garage."

We can put in time and effort but if we are putting time and effort into the wrong things we miss the target. Remember our discussion about what you need and what that would look like. Communication is so important.

Using the same scenario.

Bill gets up early and asks Mary what her plans are for the day.

Mary replies "no real plans at this time, what about you?"

Bill replies "Well, I thought I would go out and mow the lawn, clean up the yard and garage."

Mary: "that is great Bill but maybe we could hang out a bit first, have a coffee, sit on the deck and catch up after a busy week."

Bill: "okay, that works for me too."

This may seem unrealistic, but it actually can be this simple. We get an idea in our head like mowing the lawn, cleaning the yard and the garage and it is like we have blinders on. If we share our thoughts, our plans for the day we can redirect and potentially have a better day. In this scenario, one of the points I want to make is priorities. Without communicating with our partner, we may be missing something important. Is the lawn, yard and garage a priority or is spending time with Mary a priority?

What do you need and what would that look like? Bill might have said, "I am so worked up about the long grass and the mess in the yard and garage that I just have to get on that right away, it is driving me crazy." Communicating how you feel is better than just going out and doing it. **Think about some of the mixed messages that could lead to a conflict in your marriage.**

Bill says nothing, he goes out and spends a couple hours outside mowing and cleaning while Mary is left in the house wonder what the hell is wrong now. As she overthinks and over analyzes Bill spending all this time outside avoiding her she gets so worked up and furious that she is now primed and prepped for a big fight. Bill comes in all proud of his work and efforts and Mary says "what the hell is your problem today. You just go outside and avoid me all day." There is communication and there is miscommunication. Everything we do is communication in one form or another.

I realize I am presenting a lot here, but this is real life. This is how it plays out in so many homes. Bill did not mean to upset Mary, but Bill did not communicate with Mary. Mary also did not communicate with Bill, so again, the point is to communicate. Talk about your plans, talk about what you want to do today, this weekend, next week, next month. Create a shared vision moving forward. Work hard to be on the same page. Be a team. Be a partnership.

I often suggest planning the week together. Maybe it is something you do on Sunday, maybe it is something you do on Tuesday, but you do it. You talk about what you want the week and weekend to look like. This helps you get on the same page. Let us use Bill and Mary for another example.

It is Saturday morning; Bill has been thinking about mowing the lawn all week and now is the time. One problem, he has not communicated this with Mary.

It is Saturday morning; Mary has been thinking about going to the large discount store all week and now is the time. One problem, she has not communicated this with Bill.

When they wake up they have different ideas about how the day will play out. Neither one of them is wrong in this but where they went wrong is not communicating about what they need and what that would look like.

You can almost feel the conflict coming. As they sip their morning coffee they reveal their plan for the day.

Mary: "Good morning Bill, once you have your coffee let us get ready and head over to the large discount store. I have a lot I want to pick up there today."

Bill: "What are you talking about? Have you seen the lawn? When I finish my coffee, I am going out to mow the lawn."

Mary: "You can mow the lawn anytime. We need to go to the large discount store first thing in the morning to avoid the crowds."

Bill: "No way. I have had this plan to mow the lawn all week and I want to do it now and get it out of the way."

Mary: "I have had this plan to go to the large discount store all week and I want to do it now and get it out of the way."

Think about how this conflict could have been avoided. I know it seems quite obvious, but this is how many Saturday mornings start out. Conflict that could have been avoided if they would have communicated earlier in the week about what they wanted to do on the weekend.

So, we know the solution to the problem. Awareness and a willingness to make adjustments is the strategy we want to keep in mind. We know we need to communicate more effectively in order to solve this problem. The question is, will we? As I have noted earlier in our previous discussions, awareness is great, but you have to be willing to make adjustments. Bill and Mary need to communicate more effectively earlier in the week.

If you are aware and you do nothing about it you are a big part of the problem and a big part of why things are not getting better. I am sure my stepfather knew he should have been communicating more with my mother, but he did nothing to make it better. He was too stuck in his dysfunctional patterns of behavior to make adjustments. The odd thing about this is the adjustments actually make things better for everyone involved. There is no reason not to make an adjustment when you know it can improve the relationship. We discussed not living in the past lane. We cannot live life stuck in our old patterns of behavior. We must work hard to break free from the rut we are stuck in.

If we can agree that we both want the relationship to be better than it is, we must continue to agree to do what ever we can to make things better for each other. **How can you better support your partner?**

Be curious about what they need and ask what that would look like. Gather as much information as you can so you are aware but do not stop there. Your willingness to make adjustments in your life and in your relationship will be the evidence of effort and evidence of change we want to see to remain hopeful for better days ahead.

Our shared vision moving forward, our hope for better days ahead, can be developed by discussing our hopes, dreams, and expectations for our lives. **Are you heading in the direction you hoped?**

Have you ever discussed hopes, dreams, and expectations? Often, when I ask couples this question they respond with, "no, not something that has come up. We have been focused on work, raising children, running the children to different activities, basically too caught up in the busyness of life to think about hopes, dreams, and expectations."

If we never talk about this, and things are not going in the direction we hoped they would go in there may be a build up of resentment and anger that will continue to build as we think about the loss of the things we were hoping for in our lives.

We may start to blame our partners for this loss in our lives but before we do this we must remember if we have not discussed it or effectively communicated about our hopes, dreams, and expectations, our partners may have no idea.

They do not know what they do not know. We build up resentment and anger towards someone because our lives are not headed in the direction we hoped they would, but we never told them the direction we hoped our lives would head in so really we must take responsibility for this.

This is another example of why communication is so important. We allow a build up over time due to our lack of willingness to communicate what we need and what that would look like. We use avoidant behavior as our coping strategy and never seek out a solution to the problem. We just exist within a relationship, hoping for the best.

Remember what we discussed about hoping for the best. This does not get you anywhere. We need to be proactive and take initiative. If you have not had this discussion regarding hopes, dreams, and expectations for your life, you should have it soon. Do not let the build up of resentment and anger continue to consume you, because you have not put in the time and effort to discuss it.

Keep in mind that in a relationship, as long as you have a shared vision moving forward, it is okay to go down one path before heading down another. In other words, sometimes it may be going their way before it goes your way. This is the give and take and compromise part of any relationship and this is okay. We just want to make sure we get our turn when the time comes, but we will miss our turn all together if we have not communicated what we need and what that would look like. **What are your hopes, dreams, and expectations for your life and for your marriage?**

The last area of concern that I would like to discuss regarding my work with couples is family and friends. As noted earlier, communication, finances, lost hopes, dreams, and expectations are the more common areas discussed during our sessions. These areas tend to drive a wedge between a couple. Family and friends is similar. Often family and friends drive a wedge between the couple and contribute to the couples' conflicts that need to be worked through.

This becomes a complex and layered exercise in relationship dynamics and establishing healthy boundaries.

Think about your life. Think about the relationships in your life. You have family, friends, coworkers, acquaintances', neighbours, etc....

A lot of moving parts here. Relationship dynamics are complex. We establish healthy boundaries to guard against negativity that may come in and undermine our successes. We need to assess the relationships in our lives and determine whether they are healthy and helpful or unhealthy and harmful. Not always an easy task, especially when you are talking about family.

Unfortunately, family seem to be one of the most common areas of concern when discussing boundaries and wedges that get driven between a couple.

There is the mother son dynamic, which I am sure many women could speak volumes about. The mother keeps mothering her son even after he is married with children. The son continues to be mothered. When decisions need to be made the son looks to his mother for approval instead of his wife.

Genesis 2:24 "Therefore, shall a man leave his father and his mother, and shall cleave unto his wife: and they shall be one flesh." Once we are married we need to break away from our mothers and our fathers and focus on building our new life.

Our new life with our partner. When parents, whether it is the mother or the father, interfere with the daily ups and downs of our lives, there will be trouble. We lean on our parents for support but do not ever let them override the decisions you and your partner have agreed upon. That, as we say in the counseling business, would be a recipe for disaster.

Let us use Bill and Mary one last time to nail this point home regarding family and friends and the importance of establishing healthy boundaries.

Bill and Mary have an important decision to make regarding their desire to start a family.

Bill: "Hey Mary I talked to my mother about our discussion we had last night about starting a family and she thinks we may be rushing into this without thoroughly thinking it through."

Mary: "Excuse me. You did what?"

Bill: "Yeah, I talked to my mother last night….

Mary: "I heard what you said. I just cannot believe you would involve your mother in our decisions about starting a family."

Bill: "Well why not. I always talk to my mother about big decisions in my life."

Mary: "Big decisions in your life? Or is this about a big decision in our lives and it is about us, not your mother or your father or your friend or the guy down the street."

Bill: "I just thought it would be helpful to get her advice."

Mary: "We are a team, partners, sharing a vision for what we want moving forward. This is about us and no one else. We are adults who can make decisions about what is going to be best for us as a couple. No one knows our relationship as well as we do, so we are the ones that will make decisions about our relationship."

Whether it is about starting a family, buying a new house, car, boat, changing careers and so on, our relationship will get into trouble if you reach outside of our relationship for advice. I am not suggesting we never do this. I am suggesting you keep your discussions private and confidential and if it has been agreed upon to share your discussions with others than that is a different story.

For example.

Bill: "Hey Mary, I was thinking about talking to my mother about our discussion regarding starting a family. What are your thoughts?"

Communication is so important. Whether Mary says yes, or no is not the point. The point is, Bill had a discussion with his wife. He included her. This is not a case of asking for permission. It is about having a discussion. More communication leads to less conflicts.

Remember, this is a partnership. You are a team. A good team has common goals and works together to achieve those goals. A good team must communicate all the time to make sure they are on the same page moving forward.

Too often we make assumptions about what people may think, what they may feel and what they may do. Based on these assumptions we avoid conversation that we should be having. Bill should have and could have talked to Mary but most likely based on his assumption about how she would react he chose to avoid the conversation all together.

When we work hard to minimize assumptions we make in our lives, we also minimize the avoidant behaviors we have in our lives. The environment you have created with your partner, with your family and with your inner circle should be a safe place to discuss your thoughts feelings and emotions.

Earlier in the book I mentioned that I would discuss your inner circle later. Let us do that now.

Your inner circle is your family and friends who are supportive, loving, caring, and encouraging. We need to be careful who we allow in this inner circle. We are not obligated to have family members or friends in our inner circle if they are critical, judgmental, negative, and undermining our successes. Again, we need to be aware of who they are and how they are and make appropriate adjustments to keep the right people in our circle.

This obviously leads to boundaries. Making sure we establish good healthy boundaries to keep the good in and the bad out. What is good and healthy for us gets to come in. What is bad and unhealthy must stay out. This includes family members; this include friends you may have had since kindergarten. Make decisions that will be best for you, for your family and for your physical and mental health. You are allowed to establish boundaries. You are allowed to do what is best for you.

Another scenario that often comes up, which again involves our parents and their involvement in our relationship, is when we are in conflict with our partner, and we discuss this conflict with our mother or father.

I fully understand why we do this but caution you not to. When we discuss too much of our personal business, with our parents, we are blurring the lines, busting through a boundary that we should have established long ago.

We establish healthy boundaries to allow our relationship to be independent from family and friends. When we share our issues, problems, and concerns, we are inviting them into our bubble.

As I said, I understand why we do this. We are frustrated, hurt, confused, and sometimes scared. The problem I have experienced working with clients is once we tell parents, family or friends about our issues, problems and concerns they hold that story within their memories. As time goes by you may have resolved many of the issues, problems and concerns with your spouse and have moved on, but often your family and friends are still operating based on the old story and not the new one (remember old story vs new story).

If we have not updated everyone on our situation, they will be operating based on the old story and not the new one. This means you will have to update everyone you communicated with every time the story changes. This already sounds exhausting and overwhelming. I think you would agree that it would be better to create a safe environment within your relationship so you can privately discuss your areas of concern with each other and not overly involve family and friends.

We discussed resentment and anger. This happens with family and friends, and it is often directed at your spouse due to the information they are carrying around. Again, I would caution against oversharing your personal issues, problems and concerns with family and friends.

Moving on from this I would like to let you know that there will be a follow up book that will feature Bill and Mary as they continue to work through their relationship dynamics. There is a lot to talk about and a lot of helpful strategies that will be very helpful for you.

As I have often said throughout this book, if you are willing to put in the time and effort I truly believe there is nothing you cannot achieve. If a couple is willing to put in the time and effort to make their relationship better, than they will be able to make their relationship better. There is always hope as long as we see evidence of an effort and evidence of change.

CONCLUSION

I have provided my background to get us here. My journey through school and football and the lessons learned along the way. Also, my journey as a teacher, counselor, administrator, and psychologist. As I mentioned, communication is particularly important. We communicate so others may understand, and we want to build understanding to gain support. If you understand my story, if you understand the stories of others, you are better equipped to be on board and be supportive.

I have found that building rapport with students and clients has been the most important part of the working relationship I could do in the initial stages of supporting them. Building rapport with my readers is also important as my hope is some of the strategies discussed here will help you and your loved ones to have a better life and stop living in the past lane.

As the title of this book suggests, 'Living in the Past Lane', Learning how to Focus Forward, is a journey about focusing forward on better days ahead. Knowing where we came from, and remembering the challenges we have navigated through, can provide the evidence we need to find success or at least provide some level of understanding of what we can do differently to make things better.

Reviewing some of our discussion and key points. In North America, the majority of us have become accustomed to the fast pace of life. Some may even thrive on the fast pace as they face their daily routines head on or with "No Fear" as the popular slogan used to read. However, during childhood or adolescence a growing number of individuals have developed what is called Social Phobia or Social Anxiety. The two terms are interchangeable but for the purpose of this book the term Social Anxiety has been used.

Social Anxiety coupled with adolescence, often the most challenging stage of development we may ever encounter, leaves individuals literally living life in fear; fear of being noticed, fear of being embarrassed, and fear of being mocked or evaluated. This fear even extends to the anticipation of an event or situation. Social anxiety during adolescence can take an already turbulent phase of development and make it unbearable.

Fast forward to adulthood and here we are, finding ourselves struggling with similar issues and concerns related to being judged and criticized. Add a global pandemic and the conditioned behavior of withdrawing, isolating, and avoiding others and instead of focusing forward on better days ahead we find ourselves focused on the past lane. Focused on what was instead of what is and what will be.

It is not hard to predict a wave of anxiety washing over us as we reengage with society after over a year of being told not too. We must all work hard to focus forward, focus on where we are and where we are going. Remember if we are focused on the rear-view mirror all we will see is where we were and we will definitely miss where we are and/or where we are going.

We cannot let the past consume our present and disrupt our hopes for the future. This is a fight that must be fought each day. Sometimes when you feel like curling up and staying in bed the best thing to do is the opposite. Get up, get out, and engage with others.

Everyday we have choices we can make. We can redirect or reframe situations throughout our day. We are in more control than we realize. Thought life is very powerful and as we have discussed throughout this book, thought life can have a negative or a positive impact on your emotions and behaviors. **What will you do differently to make things better for you?**

Anxiety and living in the past, trips us up. Depression, feeling low, unmotivated, no drive, no interest in anything related to engaging with the world, is also a very heavy feeling many struggle with.

It is very important to be aware, and as we have discussed evidence throughout this book, remember that the evidence we chose to gather will have an impact on our emotions and behaviors.

When we are in a low, depressed mood, we seek out evidence to support how we are feeling. This awareness can help you dig yourself out. Remember awareness and then a willingness to make adjustments is an effective strategy you can use to help you get to a better place.

If I am in a negative space and feel like the world is against me, I will seek out evidence to support how I am feeling. There becomes an accumulation of evidence that I will gather throughout my day. We must fight back against this. Again, awareness (I am aware that I am not in a good place right now), what will I do? Often doing the opposite is effective.

If I am focused on the negative I must pivot and focus on the positive. It is there if you look for it. I had a client ask me if people wake up happy. I said I am not sure if everyone wakes up happy but if they do not they have choices they can make to turn things around. This is the control over your emotions and behaviors I want you to embrace. You have choices and you need to make the choices that best serve you. No one wants to be anxious, and no one wants to be depressed.

I hear it all the time. "I do not want to feel this way, but I do not have the energy to pull myself up from this." Call a friend, lean on a resource in your life, reach out to someone in your inner circle and tell them you are stuck and need some help. It is okay to ask for help. We all go through this from time to time and sometimes we need a push to get out of the rut we have fallen into.

Remember we discussed an accumulation over time, pebbles in the bucket. We must pay attention as the pebbles are going in and do something about it before they fill the bucket and spill out. Awareness and a willingness to make adjustments.

We enter relationships with many different stories. In other words, our baggage from the past. We discussed taking what is useful from the past and bringing it forward and leaving behind the baggage that trips us up and undermines our efforts to achieve success.

Visualize this. You load up the truck with your baggage. You start your journey forward. As you are driving the negative, hurtful parts of your life tumble off the back of the truck and roll into the ditch. Do you stop and pick it up? No, you keep driving. Let it go. It has no value in your life. If we live life in the past lane we stay there. If we focus forward on better days ahead we arrive in a better place.

Part of our discussions regarding relationships and couples included the understanding of what it is you are doing within the relationship to undermine its success or contribute to making it better. What are you doing differently to make it better? What can you do as a couple to better support each other? It is not a competition to see who is better. It is important to help each other be better. Set each other up for success, not failure. Appreciate your partner for who they are and how they are.

We used Bill and Mary as a way to demonstrate some of the dysfunctional interactions within a relationship and highlight the importance of effectively communicating what you need and what that would look like. My next book 'Killing the Toaster' will continue with Bill and Mary as they venture off on vacation. A continuation of highlighting the importance of communication and managing resentment and anger within a relationship.

'Killing the Toaster' will also be a continuation of our discussion regarding anxiety and depression and strategies to help you within your relationship. Remember that anxiety often presents as anger, and we must correctly identify what is going on so we can find solutions to the problem rather than add fuel to the fire. Bill may not be "always angry", he may be battling anxiety that presents as anger.

FINAL RANT

Of course, if I could go back in time, I would do some things differently.

I would have focused more on school, and my education if I only would have realized how important it would be. Yes, adults always tell us, but we do not listen because we are too young to comprehend the value of education and the wisdom of the adults trying to help us.

So, for sure, if I could go back in time, I would have focused on my education. Education is the foundation, the ultimate investment in ourselves and just to clarify, not all education we get happens in school. We have an opportunity every day to learn. We should be lifelong learners. Remember, live, and learn from our past experiences and do a better job moving forward.

I would have minimized or even eliminated the negative distractions that kept knocking me off track. As you have read, there was always something waiting for me to trip over. I call this life. Life is not easy, and it will throw you a curveball when you least expect it, but maybe that is a good thing, not a bad thing.

I believe we can learn more from our mistakes and setbacks than from our successes and achievements. Obviously, we learn from both but those mistakes we have made and the choices we make to correct or redirect our paths, I believe, have more of an impact on us. We have all made mistakes and we will continue to make mistakes. The most important thing to do after a mistake is correct the mistake. Learn from the mistake and do something different to make it better. Your true character will be revealed by this choice you make.

I would have accepted earlier in my life that everything happens for a reason. The good, the bad, and the ugly. Everything happens for a reason. This is hard to hear, hard to accept, and hard to live with when you are consumed with negativity. When all you see is the negativity and when someone comes around and tells you that everything happens for a reason, you hear the words but do not understand the point.

Why do bad things happen to good people? I suggest asking yourself, what is the lesson we are supposed to take from this, rather than dwelling on why bad things happen to good people? Focus on what it is we can learn from this.

Karma is an interesting subject area that comes up often. I would have believed more in this concept. I heard the phrase, "karma is circling the earth and taking care of business". Such a powerful statement. I have learned over the years that you get what you give, and life is a marathon, not a sprint.

Be in the here and now, be present, be aware, but look forward to the bigger picture, the idea of better days ahead, the place you hope to land. Do not fear setting short-term, mid-term, and long-term goals. Everything happens for a reason, and we need to live and learn from the past and do a better job moving forward. Be patient, even when it feels impossible to be patient.

> *"I would rather go all in on something and fail then take the easy road and always wonder what if."*

I was not the best baseball player, I was not the best hockey player, I was not the best football player, I may not have been the best, but I did my best every day.

I was not the best student, I was not the best teacher, I was not the best counsellor, and I may not the best psychologist, but I try to do my best every day.

I am the best one to write this book, to tell you my story and to share the lived experiences of others. I am the expert on my experiences and the stories I carry with me. You are the experts in your lives, you are the experts in your relationships. No one knows your life better than you. No one knows your relationships better than you.

Its not about secrets to success, secrets to love, secrets to better relationships, secrets to happiness or secrets to 'you fill in the blank', because I am sure you have seen this all before on the bookshelves.

You have everything you need within you. **What can you do differently to make things better for you?** This has been a key concept throughout this book. **What can you do differently to make things better for you? What can you and your partner do differently to better support and love each other? What can a family do differently to make things better for each other, to better support each other, to better love each other?** Not a secret, but a question that you can answer.

Be more curious about what you can do differently. Remember if nothing changes nothing changes. If we focus too much on the past, we are stuck there. Do not live life in the past lane. Take what you need from the past (the lessons learned) and pack it up and bring it forward and leave the rest behind.

We do not need to carry around extra, heavy baggage that will only weigh us down and wear us out. Let it go. Do not live life looking in the rear-view mirror because all you will see and all you will focus on is where you have been. Keep your eyes and your focus forward. Tear off the rear-view mirror, look forward, focus forward, and enjoy your journey to a better life. If you do not pay attention to where you are going, you will end up somewhere you did not want to be. Focus forward. Do not live life in the past lane.

Write your story from this point forward. At the beginning of this book, I asked you to write down your birthday. I wanted you to write your birthdate down on a piece of paper and to take a good look at that date. It was the most important date in your life. I asked you to value that date and value yourself. You are here for a reason, and I wanted to help you identify that reason.

Now I want you to write down todays date. It is the most important date in your life. Value that date and value yourself. You are here for a reason, and I want you identify your reasons. I want you to write a new story for yourself, a story that leaves all the negative, the bad, and the ugly behind.

You do not need all the negative baggage from the past tripping you up on this next phase of your journey. Take the good, the positive, and the beautiful, and carry it forward. You are here for a reason, and now you are better equipped to understand that reason and move forward with the confidence to live your best life.

I will not grieve the loss of what should have been and live life in the past lane. Instead, I will focus forward on what I have to gain in the life that I have left to live. My gain in my professional life is helping others think about their lives in a different way, a better way. Again, instead of focusing on what you may lose, focus instead on what you have to gain. Moving forward without all the baggage.

STRATEGIES

Take inventory of your thoughts and change them.

Awareness and a willingness to make adjustments. Being aware is one thing but more importantly is the willingness to make adjustments.

What can you do differently to make things better for you? When you are in a better place you are better equipped to cope and manage with the challenges of life we often are tripping over.

I talk to clients about being curious, looking for defining moments in life to help them gain a better understanding of why they are the way they are. This curiosity leads to the development of a better understanding.

When working with my clients I talk about creating a blueprint for success. Paying attention and taking note of the things that are going well in their lives and documenting these things. Things like how they react, how they respond to others, who they are with, what activities are they engaged in and so on. Basically, documenting why things are going well at that time. This is your blueprint for success. These are things you want to remember so when things go sideways you have a better idea of what you can do to pull yourself back on track, rather than continue your slide deeper into a pool of negativity.

I say to my clients "sometimes you have to look over the fence and down the road to see what is there instead of focusing on the here and now". Imagine this, you are sitting in your backyard, and you have a fence all around your yard. All you really see is the fence. In other words, all you get to see is what is right in front of you and if that is not good then all you see is bad stuff, the negative.

If you are not careful, you become consumed with negativity but remember a strategy we mentioned earlier, awareness and a willingness to make an adjustment. If you have an opportunity to look over the fence and down the street you open up opportunities to bring in new information that may help you. Be aware and then make adjustments. I believe there is always hope for better days, sometimes you just have to fight harder to see the light at the end of the tunnel or look over the fence down the street to see what else may be going on.

Live and learn from the past and try to do a better job moving forward.

We want to dispute negativity with evidence it will be okay.

Working with clients I stress the importance of having balance in their lives, work hard to provide for your families but make sure you have some balance. We work to live, not live to work.

Using techniques from CBT we discussed thoughts, feelings, and behaviors. Dispute negative thoughts with evidence it will be okay. Track thoughts and symptoms and use this documentation to make adjustments. Thinking about what we can do differently to make things better.

You will define your success in your own way. That is not for me or anyone else to decide. You, yourself, will define your own success in your own way. Some paths are gravel, and some are pavement but either way stay focused forward on better days ahead and continue to do the things you need to do to arrive at your destination.

We are not in denial that there has been negativity in our lives. We want to address these concerns, determine whether they are accurate or not and then either way, look at our recent evidence in our lives to dispute the negativity. We want to dispute negativity with evidence it will be okay.

When I work with couples, I emphasize the importance of communication and use a communication, understanding, support model. It works and goes like this. I could not support you unless I understood what you were going through, and I could not understand what you are going through unless you told me. Communication leads to understanding, which leads to support.

Where do we fit in this world? Look at the world as a gigantic puzzle. Each one of us is a puzzle piece. The picture can not be completed without us, without you. Some of us may be on the edges and some of us may be right in the middle, but either way the picture cannot be completed without us. We may play a different role and that is okay because regardless of our role we have value in the big picture. This concept may be extremely useful when someone is feeling alone, sad, depressed and wondering where they fit in this world and whether its worth continuing in this world.

NOTE: I get that there could be a counter argument to the things I am saying. My point is what are we focused on. What are we carrying forward? Do not live life in the past lane when there is so much more to look forward to.

My main goal in life right now, through my private practice and writing this book and the ones to follow, is to support people in any way that I can. I want to provide support for people, so they do not feel alone, sad, depressed, or nervous, worried, and anxious.

I believe you get what you give. I believe we should do the right things at the right times and not just because Karma is circling the earth but because kindness is what we should all be focused on. What can I do differently to make things better? What can you do differently to make things better?

QUESTIONS TO FOLLOW UP ON

What can you do differently to make things better for you?

What stands out for you? What defining moments can you make note of?

What can you put down on your blueprint for success?

Are there people in your life you need to reconnect with?

Is something from your past holding you back from enjoying your life in the here and now and holding you back from embracing thoughts about happiness in the future? Write down your thoughts on this.

What can you do differently to make your loved ones feel like they are a priority?

Are the memories you have chosen to carry forward helping you or hurting you in your quest for a happy life?

What are you doing to make your child or teenager feel like they belong in your home?

What story will you write?

Is there someone in your life that you have been shutting down, shutting out?

What is your most recent evidence telling you?

What would you put on your vision board?

What evidence can you bring forward to help you dispute negativity you are faced with today?

Who do you have in your life and what do you have in your life that keeps you going?

What can you let fall away so you can better embrace where you are or where you are headed?

Are you focused too much on the past and on what should have been or are you learning to focus forward on better days ahead?

What is your every thing will be okay song?

What are your hopes, dreams, and expectations for the story you are writing?

When we dwell on negativity it changes how we feel and how we behave. Can you recall a time when you have done this?

What issues, problems or concerns are tripping you up daily?

What evidence have you found in your inventory of successes and achievements?

What can you embrace to help you pull yourself up and out of your pool of negativity?

What can you do differently today within your daily routine to make things better for you?

What can you do differently throughout your week to make things better for you?

What thoughts are keeping you stuck in the past? What thoughts are helping you dispute the negativity from the past?

Are you operating in the here and now or speeding down the road in the past lane?

Assess your self-talk so you can determine if it is helpful or hurtful.

What have you discovered about your defining moment or defining moments in your life?

What is the one thing you can do differently today, this week, this month, to make things better for you?

What is the one thing we can do differently to better support each other?

What is it that you need and what does that look like?

How can you better support your partner?

Are you heading in the direction you hoped?

What are your hopes, dreams, and expectations for your life and for your marriage?

Now is the time to write your new story. What is your new story?

CONCLUDING OUR DISCUSSION

Here is another interesting area I wanted to discuss as we wrap up this discussion. Whether you are religious or not I want you to have an open mind and try and appreciate this for what it is. Our world right now is spiralling into a pool of negativity.

Below I have listed the ten commandments from the bible. Now as I said, try and have an open mind. If it helps you, skip over the first three.

Take a look at number four to number ten. What if we followed these rules? What would our world look like? How much better off would we be? That is all I really wanted to say with regards to this. Try and think about things in a different way. What ifs do not always have to be about the doom and gloom, or when will the other foot drop. What ifs can be exciting and amazing. What if we followed some of the rules listed below...

The ten commandments, in order, are:

1. *"I am the Lord thy God, thou shalt not have any strange gods before Me."*
   This commandment forbids idolatry, the worship of false gods and goddesses, and it excludes polytheism, the belief in many gods, insisting instead on monotheism, the belief in one God.

2. *"Thou shalt not take the name of the Lord thy God in vain."*
   The faithful are required to honor the name of God. It makes sense that if you're to love God with all your heart, soul, mind, and strength, then you're naturally to respect the name of God with equal passion and vigor.

3. *"Remember to keep holy the Sabbath day."*
    The Jewish celebration of Sabbath (Shabbat) begins at sundown on Friday evening and lasts until sundown on Saturday. Catholic, Protestant, and Orthodox Christians go to church on Sunday, treating it as the Lord's Day instead of Saturday to honor the day Christ rose from the dead.

4. *"Honor thy father and mother."*
    This commandment obliges the faithful to show respect for their parents — as children and adults. Children must obey their parents, and adults must respect and see to the care of their parents, when they become old and infirm.

5. *"Thou shalt not kill."*
    The better translation from the Hebrew would be "Thou shalt not murder" — a subtle distinction but an important one to the Church. Killing an innocent person is considered murder. Killing an unjust aggressor to preserve your own life is still killing, but it is not considered murder or immoral.

6. *"Thou shalt not commit adultery."*
    The sixth and ninth commandments honor human sexuality. This commandment forbids the actual, physical act of having immoral sexual activity, specifically adultery, which is sex with someone else's spouse or a spouse cheating on their partner.

7. *"Thou shalt not steal."*
    The seventh and tenth commandments focus on respecting and honoring the possessions of others. This commandment forbids the act of taking someone else's property. Embezzlement, fraud, tax evasion, and vandalism are all considered extensions of violations of the Seventh Commandment.

8. *"Thou shalt not bear false witness against thy neighbor."*
    The Eighth Commandment condemns lying. Because God is
    regarded as the author of all truth, the Church believes that
    humans are obligated to honor the truth. The most obvious way
    to fulfill this commandment is not to lie — intentionally deceive
    another by speaking a falsehood.

9. *"Thou shalt not covet thy neighbor's wife."*
    The Ninth Commandment forbids the intentional desire and
    longing for immoral sexuality. To sin in the heart, Jesus says, is to
    lust after a woman or a man in your heart with the desire and will
    to have immoral sex with them. Just as human life is a gift from
    God and needs to be respected, defended, and protected, so, too, is
    human sexuality.

10. *"Thou shalt not covet thy neighbor's goods."*
    The Tenth Commandment forbids the wanting to or taking some-
    one else's property. Along with the Seventh Commandment, this
    commandment condemns theft and the feelings of envy, greed, and
    jealousy in reaction to what other people have.

SUPPORTING MENTAL HEALTH

Life in the Past Lane -
Focus Forward / Better Days Ahead

Highlighting one of the key concepts from the book Life in the Past Lane, Focus Forward and Better Days Ahead products have been created to support mental health and a path to a better life.

https://life-in-the-past-lane.myshopify.com/